The GREATEST
in the WORLD

illustrated by
Graham Kennedy

Malcolm Boyden

The Greatest
Podcasting
Tips in the World

A 'The Greatest in the World' book

www.thegreatestintheworld.com

Illustrations:
Graham Kennedy
gkillus@aol.com

Cover & layout design:
the designcouch
www.designcouch.co.uk

Cover images:
© Scott Frangos; © Oleg Kulakov; © Vanessa Martineau; © Bruce Parrott
all courtesy of www.fotolia.com

Copy editor:
Bronwyn Robertson
www.theartsva.com

Series creator/editor:
Steve Brookes

First published in 2007 by Public Eye Publications

This edition published in 2007 by
The Greatest in the World Ltd., PO Box 3182
Stratford-upon-Avon, Warwickshire CV37 7XW

Text and illustrations copyright © 2007 – The Greatest in the World Ltd.

A CIP catalogue record for this book is available from the British Library
ISBN 978-1-905151-75-2

Printed and bound in China by 1010 Printing International Ltd.

Dedicated to the world's
newest batch of broadcasting legends –
most of whom will be created by this book.

Contents

Introduction ...

Wouldn't it be great if you could create your very own radio station? If you could broadcast your radio shows across the whole world? If you could show off your talent on a global stage? If you could earn a lucrative living from the pulsating world of the professional broadcaster? If you could deliver your message, whatever it is, to a global audience at the touch of a button? Well, I've got some exciting news ... It's all well within your grasp, and it's much easier than you think. In fact, together we're going to make it happen.

Welcome to the dawn of a new broadcasting era. If you like, it's a radio revolution and it's starting now. It's the breakthrough the broadcasting industry has been waiting for. The breakthrough that will change the world of radio forever. The biggest breakthrough since the golden age of the old-fashioned wireless. The breakthrough that could turn you into a radio star. The breakthrough that may well earn you fame and fortune.

The breakthrough that means we can all now broadcast our own radio programmes, on our own radio stations, direct to listeners, around the whole world ... And we don't even have to leave the comfort of our front room. The breakthrough that is ... Podcasting.

I've written this book with the aim of creating many hundreds of new, talented broadcasters and entertainers right across the globe. I've put it together to present you with a 'once in a lifetime' opportunity. If you like, it's the key that will unlock your broadcasting talents.

Outlining dozens of inspirational ideas, this book is specifically designed to start you off on an exciting new journey. Together we'll make our first tentative steps into the exciting world of podcasting. We'll learn what it's all about and how to do it! Before long we'll be taking giant strides into unclaimed territory. Ultimately, you could become a broadcasting giant.

It's new, it's easy, and it's exciting. Hold on tight – and enjoy the adventure!

Good luck!

chapter 1
Welcome to the revolution

Watch out world… here I come!

Have you got something to say? Has it always been your passion
to move into the exciting world of the professional broadcaster?
Would you like to have your own radio show on your own station
that broadcasts, not to a specific region, but to the whole world?
Do you want to make a business out of your broadcasting talents?

If the answer is yes … read on …

Hold on a minute – what is podcasting?

Where have you been? Alright, I forgive you. The term
'podcasting' was only coined in 2004, although it became
America's Word of the Year in 2005 – an accolade bestowed
upon it by the New Oxford American Dictionary.

What's in a word?

The term 'podcasting' can be confusing. It originates from the
combination of the words 'iPod' and 'broadcast'. Although you
don't necessarily need an iPod to listen to podcasts, the name
caught on through convenience (and the fact that nobody could
think of anything more dynamic!).

For want of a better phrase, people began to latch onto it, and,
like any popular nickname, it's stuck!

The history lesson – in seven quick steps

1. In the beginning there were computers. Then, man said "Let's create a worldwide web!"

2. Web sites began to appear on the Internet – and then blog sites (a special kind of website, containing a person's journal or online personal diary). Blogs are arranged in reverse chronological order with the most recent post at the top.

3. Bloggers got bored of just writing their thoughts down, so they developed a way to broadcast them to the world … audioblogging or podcasting was born! The first podcasts began to emerge in 2003.

4. Podcasting moved on! From the early seeds, new websites and software support began to sprout up everywhere. RSS feeds were discovered which meant that broadcasts could be delivered DIRECT to anyone, anywhere in the world.

5. The podcast explosion began.

6. You burst onto the podcasting scene and things really started to happen.

7. The future? Write it yourself, if you like!

Radio magic

Podcasting involves you creating your very own radio show (podcast) that can be listened to by anyone in the world on a computer / MP3 player / iPod or almost any other kind of portable audio device.

In the next decade or so, experts are predicting that it could easily overtake conventional radio as the world's main source of broadcasting. To put it simply, podcasts are radio shows on the Internet. What makes them special is how they get delivered to the listener. (You'll read about that later.)

Who can podcast?

Anyone with a mouth ... as long as you can make a sound from it!

Who can listen?

Everyone! As long as they've got computer, iPod or MP3 player. Right now there are hundreds of new radio shows catering for thousands of different tastes. Listeners just have to pick a show that takes their fancy, subscribe to it ... and listen! Every day more and more listeners are letting new broadcasters into their lives. Every day broadcasters are picking up new fans from all around the world.

Re-inventing the wheel

Podcasting is at the cutting, thrusting edge of a new broadcasting era.

For the budding broadcaster, it's your chance to be heard throughout the world. Your once in a lifetime opportunity to send your message (whatever it may be) to the globe – made from home, on your very own radio station.

For the listener – podcasting marks the beginning of a brand new, thrilling period – for the first time they can listen to exactly what they want to hear, when they want to hear it.

Listeners can now choose radio shows devoted to their specific interests, and when they subscribe to your radio show, they get it delivered to them direct, free of charge, wherever they are in the world. Furthermore, they get every new episode automatically.

Magical isn't it?

And here's the best bit

Because it's so new, podcasting immediately catapults you onto a level playing field with the big boys of the industry – the broadcasting legends. Congratulations! You are now standing shoulder to shoulder with your radio heroes.

But it's all too technical … isn't it?

No.

Go on then, convince me!

If you're not very technical, then welcome to the club. We don't do geek speak in this book! I'm probably the least technically-minded person you could ever meet, yet later on I'll take you, step by step, through the process of making a podcast ... your very own radio show on your very own radio station.

It's easy to create a podcast. Much easier for you to do than for me to explain. Anyone can podcast within a few minutes. If you have a computer and an Internet hook-up, your radio station is almost built and ready to broadcast – as long as you are ready and willing to speak to the globe.

Don't get grabbed by the technicals

Podcasting is for broadcasters and entertainers ... not for techno-bores! This book is written from a broadcaster's point of view. You could spend hours trudging through technical websites, getting bogged down by what equipment to use and how to use it. The cost of your microphone, the size of your mixing desk and the depth of your computer knowledge is of little consequence. It's the broadcaster that matters: what you're saying and how you're delivering your message. Think of podcasting simply as a tool to promote your talent.

Remember

It doesn't matter if you're a technical genius ... if you're not a budding broadcaster with a passion to get your message heard by the world, then podcasting is not for you. Of course, having some technical knowledge will help. But it's by no means vital. Don't get put off by the technicals! I'd rather you be a technophobe than a techno-bore!

Imagine this …

1. You can now share your views with the world on your very own radio station.

2. People can listen to you wherever they are in the world – whenever the fancy takes them.

3. Listeners around the world can subscribe to your show free of charge. Once they've subscribed, your shows are automatically downloaded and updated so your new growing band of followers won't miss a thing.

4. When your broadcast becomes popular, your loyal band of fans might even be happy to pay to subscribe to your show and hear your words of wisdom!

In the driving seat

Podcasting is the future.

If the broadcasting industry makes you tick, podcasting will transform you from an also-ran … into a front-runner. Hopefully, this book will help you turn your broadcasting dreams into reality. Together, we'll endeavour to turn your hobby into a rewarding career. Furthermore, the awesome predictions in this book will help map out a glowing, yet radical, path for the broadcast business worldwide.

Remember

You can record a podcast on literally any subject you like. If you've got something to say … why not say it to the whole world?

The world is waiting … what are you waiting for?

Leading the way

Wake up! Podcasting can turn anybody and everybody into worldwide radio stars. It's my aim to give you the knowledge and encouragement to become a leading light in the broadcast revolution.

And don't let anybody tell you that podcasting isn't 'real broadcasting'.

It's happening!

Broadcasting is buzzing – and the boardroom gossip is all about 'social media' and 'user-generated content' ... that simply involves normal folk like you and me making exciting radio for other normal folk ... Like you and me.

And it's all being made possible thanks to the podcasting revolution.

A 2007 survey revealed that 70% of senior executives in the media and entertainment business are predicting a social media (or people power) explosion in the next three years. Only 3% saw podcasting as a passing fad.

It's predicted that by 2010, 12.3 million households in the United States will be listening to podcasts as their main source of audio entertainment.

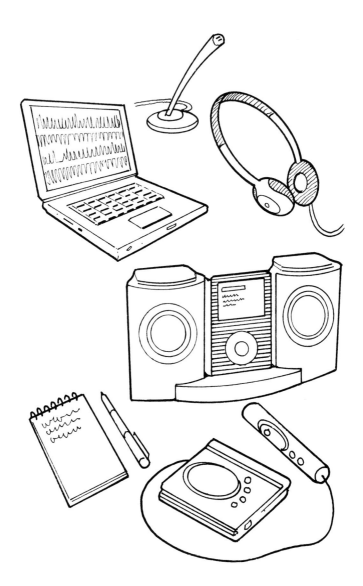

chapter 2
Your slice of radio heaven

What kit do I need?

1. **A computer!** Nearly all PCs have an adequate soundcard for podcasting – if not, you can easily upgrade. Similarly, if your computer is getting on a bit and runs at a snail's pace, just add some more memory (RAM) which should do the trick nicely.

2. **A microphone**. Good quality microphones are becoming increasingly available off the shelf.

3. **A computer programme**. To record your voice and, if necessary, edit the recording – cutting out any mistakes and adding a few exciting effects. There are loads of free ones available on the Internet, some of which are also used by top professionals.

4. **A selection of software** – easy to download and often free –to convert your show into an MP3 recording and upload it to the Internet.

5. **A website or blog** on which to air your radio show. It's your shop window to listeners around the globe.

6. **Headphones** are a nice option, especially if you want to hear your show played back without the additional noise of a desktop speaker. BUT they are not absolutely vital.

Your radio station is now complete!

Congratulations. You're the owner of the world's newest and most exciting radio station. You will soon be ready to broadcast to the universe!

What microphone should I use?

Microphones are available in a variety of styles, depending on your budget. Some computers already have microphones built into them. If your computer doesn't have one, or you want to use something that cancels out noise a little better and helps you sound as professional as possible, you can buy an inexpensive, good quality microphone at any office supply outlet, music store or electronics shop.

Better quality recordings will be achieved using a 'directional mic' – one that picks up noise from the source it's pointed at (i.e. your mouth!) thereby eliminating background sounds. Omni-directional mics pick up sound from all around. Shure microphones come highly recommended in the business. They are durable and relatively cheap (see if you can pick up a secondhand one on eBay!).

There are also good quality USB microphones available specifically for podcasting. These will do an excellent job for you. Don't forget, you might need two or more microphones if you plan to interview guests or talk to others on your radio show.

Headsets can be a useful podcasting tool because they are headphones and microphone combined.

Plugging in!

All standard computers have a microphone and headphone socket. A more advanced soundcard will provide you with extra user-friendly options for a variety of other inputs – this might prove easier in the long run and is well worth investigating.

Go shopping, and see what best suits your needs.

Picking your website

Ideally, your website address – or domain if you prefer to use that term – will be the same name as that of your radio station. For example, the new internet radio station, Radio Heaven can be found at **www.RadioHeaven.com**.

Have fun picking and registering your domain. It's important that you choose well. Create a name that yells "You've got to listen to this!" Often, the first thing a listener will see is the name of your radio station. Your website address is your unique brand.

Try to look for a dot-com address. The name you prefer might not be available, so you'll need to get creative – and shop around. You'll have to pay a small fee for registering your domain – but remember, it is your shop window. If you like, it's your frequency – where your radio shows can be found, and heard.

Your website will come with a full address (URL). A URL reads something like this ... **http://www.RadioHeaven.com.**

Don't worry if you don't have a website or if you prefer not to invest in one at this stage. There are a number of superb blog sites that give you your own webpage, often free of charge (you'll read more about that later).

Don't forget, blog sites began this particular radio revolution. They are still a great way to dip your toe into the podcasting pool as they take much of the technical hassle off your shoulders (you'll read about that too).

Your first radio studio

Use a spare room or your office at home. Make sure that the dog isn't barking, the kids aren't screaming in the background and the television is switched off. Also, make sure the room doesn't have too many echoes or too much reverberation when you record.

Believe it or not, your wardrobe makes an ideal radio studio! The clothes are an excellent, and attentive, audience – and they dampen the sound perfectly. Of course, the rest of your family might wonder why you've suddenly started to hide yourself away in the closet with your computer!

A small amount of attention is needed to make sure that your studio environment is ready to go. But essentially, all you need to do is shut the door, pick up the microphone ... and start talking!

What shall I talk about?

Don't worry too much about that yet. This book gives you dozens of ideas on the content and structure of your radio show. It also tells you how to become a great broadcaster.

As a general rule of thumb let me ask you one question "What interests you?" More to the point, "What are you passionate about?" Your answer could form the basis of your radio programme.

Don't just sit there and gabble on about nothing. Content is crucial – but we'll investigate that later on. For now, have fun getting to know your equipment. Practise your editing and become comfortable with your own presentation style.

Watch your pocket

Don't break the bank trying to create your mini-podcast empire; start off small and with the minimum expense. There is simply no need to spend a lot of money on an expensive microphone or high-end sound mixing equipment at first. As your podcasting career becomes more serious, you can then slowly begin to invest in better equipment.

Your computer programme

Next, you'll need to download a programme that records your voice, ideally one with an audio editor, so you can play around with your recording ... and cut out your mistakes!

The audio editing software, Audacity, is suitable for PC and Mac. It's easy to use, it's the pick of most top professionals ... and it's FREE to download. Audacity is a great choice because it's simple for first time users, it will take you less than two minutes to download... and it's FREE. Go and download it now if you like, **http://audacity.sourceforge.net**/ ... you'll see what I mean! (And you'll have taken the first major step in your new broadcasting career.)

Of course, there are many other programmes available. Some experts will point you in the direction of Adobe Audition 2.0 (previously known as Cool Edit Pro) or ePodcast Creator. Most Mac users download Garageband, which is both powerful and free. Increasingly Garageband is making it easier for the new breed of podcast pioneers with specially designed podcast features. Have a rummage around and see which one suits you best.

Let's get started

We'll make a radio show, using Audacity, in seven magnificent, easy steps …

1. **Download.**
   If you haven't done so already, download the Audacity programme to your computer. It's free (have I mentioned that already?) and it will take only a minute or so. **http://audacity.sourceforge.net/**

2. **Testing, Testing!**
   Make sure Audacity is picking up your microphone. To do this you'll need to choose the correct input source by clicking "file" then "preferences" then "Audio I/O". You only need to configure your input source once, then you're away. You'll probably find that Audacity has already selected the correct input source for you and there's nothing to change.

3. **Record.**
   Click the button with the red circle and off you go.

4. **Talk!**
   Audacity displays sound as a 'wave form' with volume represented vertically. Loud sections show higher peaks than the quiet ones. You'll be able to adjust and monitor your levels when using Audacity. (I'll explain more about recording levels in a moment.)

5. **Stop.**
   Click the button with the yellow square.

6. **Play.**
   Click the green arrow.

7. **Celebrate!**
   You're a broadcasting legend in the making!

Editing your show

When your audio has been recorded, it can be edited. (Always remember to save your work first.)

The tool palette is in the top left hand corner. It contains six tools but for now, we only need to concentrate on three.

1. The I-bar or selection tool. Use this to select various parts of your recording in order to delete them, amplify them and so on. This is probably the tool you'll use most.

2. The time shift tool (a double ended arrow!). This enables you to grab your recording and slide it around, perhaps to fit it into a piece of music.

3. The 'zoom' tool. (A magnifying glass!) The zoom tool makes editing easier by stretching your recording vertically or horizontally to help with the more tricky editing adjustments, like disposing of a single word.

Muck about!

Have fun playing around with all the effects controls and the editing features of the programme. You can move your recording about with the time shift tool, add music by going into the "projects" tab at the top of the screen, fade music in or out by entering the "effects" tab – cut and paste – even amplify your work if it's been recorded at too low a frequency.

Oops!

One of the best aspects of Audacity is that, by accessing the "edit" tab at the top of the screen, you can "undo" your last action. So, if you delete an award-winning piece of audio by mistake then fear not, "edit" and "undo" will come to the rescue.

Remember

Audacity gives you the capability to record, amplify, echo, fade music in and out, edit and mix an unlimited amount of tracks, and features easy editing with cut, copy, paste, and delete. And, by the way, IT'S FREE!

Watch your levels

Volume levels are vitally important. If your radio show is uncomfortable to the ear – then your message will not be heard, however well delivered. If your levels are not constant, your podcast will be of no use. Keep a close eye on your volume. It's important that you record your programme loud enough for your listeners to hear but not so loud that it becomes distorted.

Always, always try to keep your volume levels constant.
To help you out, Audacity's compressor (found in the "effects" menu) is one of its most useful tools. First it gets rid of your unwanted volume peaks, then, with the loud bits gone, it raises the volume of the remaining broadcast, eliminating the quiet sections.

Have a few trial runs until you get it right.

Podcasting has no rules. Almost every day broadcasters are finding new and exciting ways to put their message across.

A golden nugget

There's a lovely, user-friendly website
www.how-to-podcast-tuturial.com, that takes you on a free
video tour of Audacity. It talks you through the process of
recording, editing, and mucking about using the programme.
Go to the "Audacity tutorial for podcasters" section –
watch, listen, and learn. The tutorial is fantastic (and free).
It's explained so easily that anyone could pick it up in an instant.
It's child's play!

Clipping and popping

These two chaps are the podcasters' arch enemy. They occur
when you have your recording levels or volume settings too high.

Clipping is another word for distortion as a result of your
recording being too loud. You hear clipping as a sharp crackling
sound.

Popping is a noise produced by the microphone when it's
struck by a puff of air that's forced out of the broadcaster's
mouth during the pronunciation of the Ps and Bs. It means
you're recording at too high a volume or you're too close to
the microphone.

Mind your Ps and Bs

It doesn't cost a great deal to buy a pop filter, which eliminates
any popping sounds. A pop filter is basically screen material
stretched over a hoop that sits in front of a microphone as you
speak into it.

What next?

So you've created your first recording and you're happy with the way you sound.

Here's what to do next:

1. After saving your show, you need to convert the broadcast to an MP3 format before you upload it to the Internet. Audacity will let you know that it needs the LAME MP3 Encoder in order to export your files as MP3s, but don't worry – this is also a simple and free download.

2. LAME actually stands for "LAME Ain't an MP3 Encoder"! But it is... and it's not lame at all – it's actually very good. Quite simply, LAME is a 'plug-in' to Audacity that allows you to convert your recording into an MP3 file. Easy!

3. Don't forget to label your MP3 file. This simply involves filling out an ID3 Tag with the name of your show, the broadcaster and your website address. You can add more information if you like, but you don't have to.

4. Finally, you'll need to upload your radio show to the Internet. This might involve downloading a File Transfer Programme (FTP). A File Transfer Programme makes it as easy as dragging and dropping! There are many FTP programmes available on the Internet and sites to help you – such as **www.smartFTP. com**. (Don't get confused! If you don't fancy delving into the world of FTP programmes, I'll tell you how to bypass the uploading process in Chapter 4).

Congratulations!

You've made your first radio show. You are now an active player in the world's latest and greatest broadcast revolution. Who told you this was too technical?

chapter 3

Fairy godmothers and woofle dust!

So, you've created your own radio show and you're up and running. How does the magic happen? Where's the woofle dust? Exactly how does your show get delivered direct to listeners around the world? You're about to find out – but first, let's ask a simple question "Why should people listen to podcasts rather than conventional radio?"

What's in it for the listener?

Imagine the weekend papers have just dropped through your letterbox. Some members of the family want the sports section. Others require the news. The children might want to read the entertainment. Everybody's different – we all like different things.

The podcast caters for people's individual tastes, delivering exactly the type of radio show they want to hear – and they can listen when the fancy takes them: in the car, on the train, while walking the dog, or in the bath.

Imagine that …

For the listeners, it's gripping stuff. It's like subscribing to your favourite magazine. You don't think about it, until the magazine drops onto the mat at the beginning of each month – but it's always a nice surprise when you hear the thud.

The delight is multiplied considerably when your personal radio show thuds onto your MP3 player / iPod or computer.

Breaking the mould

Have you ever listened to radio in the car? When you hear something that interests you, do you immediately turn the volume up? We all do it.

But very often, while listening to conventional radio, we have to sit through many hours of radio that's not applicable to our lives before we find a nugget that takes our fancy. Sometimes the volume never goes up ... and the radio gets switched off.

Either that, or you've got your finger constantly on the button flicking from station to station trying to find something of interest.

With podcasting, the content of the show is focussed entirely on the listener. It's radio heaven. And an advertiser's paradise.

Radio on demand

Only recently, a major broadcasting document focussed on the need for Radio on Demand. That's how seriously people are taking the exhilarating world of podcasting.

So let's take our first bold leap forward. When we see, hear, or read the word 'Podcast' think instead 'Rodcast' ... **R.O.D** meaning **Radio on Demand**!

There you are – we've done it! We've created a new identity for this latest broadcast phenomenon. Congratulations, you're the first of a new breed – you're leading the Radio on Demand revolution. As well as being a quality podcaster – you are also one of the world's first Radio on Demand broadcasters (or "R.o.d.Casters").

There are more than enough potential listeners out there to cope with the podcasting phenomenon.

In 2004, 800,000 people downloaded a podcast.

In 2005, that figure had grown to a staggering 4.8 million ... and we've only just scratched the surface.

Over the next few years, listeners will continue downloading and enjoying your radio shows in ever increasing numbers.

So who hears me and how?

As I've already mentioned, the magic of podcasting is the way your broadcasts get delivered to your new listeners. When you've had fun making your podcast, it gets distributed in one of two ways ...

1. The boring route! Simply upload your show directly onto your chosen website so that visitors to that website can download it at their leisure, to listen to on their own computer / Mp3 player / iPod or conventional portable CD player.

2. The exciting way! If you want to raise the bar and start becoming really professional, you can sign up, free of charge, to one of the world's podcast distributors (named 'aggregators' or 'podcatchers').

What's the difference?

A podcast posted onto your webpage is like a newspaper that sits on the shelves of the paper shop waiting to be snapped up. Listeners have to find your webpage before downloading your show – and they have to keep checking to see if you've made new shows.

Aggregators or Podcatchers will deliver the show on your behalf, direct to the listener. Furthermore, they'll automatically deliver future episodes of your show whenever they are made. Some of them also keep an archive of every radio show you've done so new listeners can catch up on what they've missed.

Aggregators are the 'paper boys' of the podcast world. They deliver your radio show to anyone in the world who wants to listen (subscribe). They also provide you with a shop window. New listeners will browse around the podcatchers' sites (they are sometimes referred to as podcast hosting sites) to decide which shows they want delivered to their computers – the ones they wish to subscribe to.

Your fairy godmothers!

Aggregators are the fairy godmothers of the podcasting world. They sprinkle 'woofle dust' onto your broadcast and make it magically appear for your new family of listeners. A good aggregator works like a satellite TV channel guide – making it easy for the broadcaster to place his show ... and the listener to simply get their hands on exactly what they want to hear.

Probably the most famous aggregator or podcatcher in the world is iTunes. Their latest directory gives listeners the chance to hear shows on almost everything at the click of a button – from animals to aviation and trucking to tattooing.

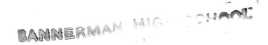

Aggregators like iTunes are the paperboys of the podcast world. They deliver your talent onto a global stage.

Which podcatcher shall I use?

As well as iTunes, there are many dozens of aggregators or podcatchers around the world catering for hundreds of different podcasts (soon there will be thousands); **ipodder.org** was one of the first and still considers itself to be one of the best. But it's by no means the only one; **http://britcaster.com** deals with the growing army of British Broadcasters.

It might be worth also trying out **www.podcastpickle.com** – an excellent site about podcasting that doesn't take itself too seriously. Other leaders in this field are **www.podcastalley.com** and **www.podcastbunker.com** – and then there's one of the originals, the superb **www.podcast.net**. There are new ones emerging every day, and some disappearing (don't forget, this is a revolution and things are changing quickly). At **www.podcastingnews.com**, they have a useful – but not exhaustive – list. They also provide good advice on all sorts of podcasting matters.

Remember

You can sign up with as many aggregators as you wish in order to give you maximum, worldwide exposure. Why not? It won't cost you a penny.

How it works

Put simply, aggregators will ask for a description of your programme (an RSS Feed) and then they'll start distributing your show anywhere in the world. They'll also start promoting your show in their podcast directories.

The RSS feed is simply a special code enabling aggregators to 'catch' any new programmes you put online and deliver them directly to your subscribers. Every time you release something new, they'll automatically receive it, promote it, and distribute it.

What does RSS stand for?

Really Simple Syndication.

And it does exactly what it says on the tin – syndicates your radio show (and your broadcasting talent) to the whole world.

Have a feed up on me!

Creating an RSS feed can seem quite daunting at first.
Don't worry – it's not! It's as simple as filling in a form on your computer, which contains the most important details about your radio station and its programmes.

To make it really easy, just download an example of someone else's RSS form, and replace their details with your own.
Don't worry, it's not cheating – everyone does it to start with!

An easy route

Before you start sweating like a glassblower's backside, relax! There are dozens of useful sites that will help you fill out an RSS feed form automatically in a matter of minutes. You don't have to be a code cracker or remember any awkward formats.

Sites like **www.feedforall.com** will do everything for you. Feedforall is one of the leading sites in this field alongside www.feedburner.com and **www.feedpublish.com**. The **www.rsscreator.com** website boasts "Just create the show and leave the coding to other guys". Other helpful websites offer examples of forms for you to download and enter your own details.

Do It Yourself

If you fancy creating your own RSS feed, here are the basics:

The ingredients you'll need to include are:

1. **A title**.
   Put simply, the name of your radio station, e.g. Radio Heaven.
2. **A link**.
   The full address (URL) of the website you want associated with the podcast, for example,
   http://www.Radioheaven.com.
3. **A description**.
   What type of programmes your radio station will be broadcasting, for example, sport, comedy, music, etc.

You may include optional extras such as language (if your broadcast is in English, the language is en-us). You could also include a publishing date and copyright information. (Don't forget, you hold the copyright to your shows because you are the talent. Always protect your work – don't let others steal your ideas!)

The bad news …

Every time you create a new radio show, you'll have to update your RSS feed with information about your latest episode so your aggregators will notice it – and distribute it to your listeners.

The good news …

The three ingredients I've just mentioned will always stay the same. Only details of your new episode change … so it won't take you very long once you've got the hang of it!

Here are the three ingredients that will change with every show:

1. **An episode title**.
   Simply enter the name of your latest radio show (not station, as above). For example "Episode one – welcome to Radio Heaven".

2. **A link**.
   Again, the full website address (URL).

3. **A description**.
   What that specific episode is about.

You might also encounter a section asking you how long your radio show is (in bytes) and what format it's in (I'd always stick to MP3).

The final step involves you validating your RSS feed with the click of a button. That's the easiest bit of all.

XML (what?)

RSS feeds are written in a language that can be read by both humans and machines called XML. Don't worry – it's only jargon and it won't affect you in the slightest.

RSS feeds are created in tags and enclosed in brackets – you'll see what I mean if you search for an example of an RSS feed.

Remember

There are sites that will help you create an RSS feed automatically, in a matter of minutes. Others give you the template to simply fill in your own information.

These sites create feeds that will be accepted by loads of different aggregators so you can have your show distributed and promoted by as many podcatchers as you like.

The more podcatchers you have, the more promotion your radio station gets around the world ... and the more listeners you'll pick up.

It's a gift

Most listeners will have your show delivered to them from an aggregator free of charge, although, when your broadcast becomes irresistible to fans the whole world over, they might be happy to pay to hear it (you'll read about that later!).

If you get a worldwide army of fans, you'll be well on the way to becoming a cult broadcaster (you'll be hearing about that as well).

Aggregators are the paper boys of the podcasting world – they manage the distribution of your show and give it valuable promotion on their directories. But they don't charge you for that service. Once you've signed up ... you're in!

You ain't heard nothing yet!

Don't forget you are a pioneer. You are at the forefront of a broadcasting revolution. Things are changing rapidly.

Technology boffins are predicting that companies will soon develop new products to make podcasting even easier. There's talk of a tool that will record and edit your show, automatically convert it to an MP3 file, and then instantly distribute it directly to your listeners and chosen aggregators ... all at the click of a button.

One company is very close to developing that tool. When it's available it will make podcasting so easy to produce and understand that the floodgates will open and the number of podcast broadcasters and listeners will explode. Luckily, you'll be in the right place – at the right time – to capitalise on the revolution.

It's happening!

In the words of a senior entertainment executive, based at the BBC in London: "Podcasting is an ever-shifting plain, but we predict it will evolve into the most serious challenge to conventional radio since the advent of television."

GONE TO MAKE A
PODCAST –
BACK IN 5 MINUTES

chapter 4
Podcasting to go!

The quick fix podcast

If you don't have a website and find the prospect of uploading your show onto the internet using a File Transfer Programme (FTP) too stressful, don't panic. Similarly, if creating RSS feeds sounds too much to take, then relax. Help is at hand.

There is an even easier way to broadcast to the world – which is just as effective and even cheaper! In fact it's perfect if you simply want to podcast for a hobby.

If you want to just concentrate on making the radio show and leave the technical stuff to the others – you can!

I call it 'Quick Fix' or 'Short Cut' podcasting.

The blog-roll!

There are dozens of blog sites that give you the chance to create, publish, listen, and subscribe to regular podcasts without spending a packet. You don't have to worry about uploading your radio show to the Internet or creating an RSS feed – you don't even need a website. Blogs give you your own webpage and do the rest for you.

Blog sites are a cheap and easy route to podcasting if you simply want to dip your toe into the magical world of broadcasting.

All you've got to do is talk!

Fed up with just putting their written thoughts onto their blog pages, early bloggers began to attach audio files. Podcasting was originally known as audio-blogging.

Even though the podcast revolution has moved on – you can still choose the blog route today to get you started; **www.audioblog.com**, **www.clickcaster.com**, **http://ourmedia.org** or **www.audioacrobat.com** are among the dozens of friendly, well-designed websites that will give you a webpage for your podcast. It will probably look like this **www.audioblog.com/your station's name**. They'll upload your audio at the click of a button and act as your podcasting host. Some will even give you an RSS file. All you have to do is grab the microphone and talk!

My Space

MySpace (**www.myspace.com**) is set to take the podcast revolution to new levels. MySpace is rapidly emerging as the top social networking blog site. Like the others, it provides you with a personal webpage (**www.myspace.com/yourstation'sname**) to create your own radio station. Once you've started recording, your audience will grow – often from word of mouth. You can upload your podcast free to **www.myspace.com**, and people can download it.

In the near future, if your shows are deemed entertaining enough, it might be possible to sell them to subscribers on MySpace. Already MySpace is becoming a great spotlight for new bands to showcase their music to the world.

The short cut to success!

With some of these shortcut sites, you don't even need to record your show with Audacity. If you are using **www.clickcaster.com**, for instance, you simply …

1. Log in. It's free!
2. Type in the title of your radio show.
3. Hit record.
4. Talk!
5. Click publish!

How easy is that! You've created your own radio show in minutes – totally hassle free.

Skype is another one of the quick-fix podcast outlets (**www.skype.com**); based in Luxemburg, Skype started life as an Internet telephone service that's now branched out into podcasting (or, as they call it 'Skypecasting'). They boast that Skypecasting is "A new way to have conversations across the world with people who share your interests"! Skypecasting is another free and easy podcasting route.

Grab a microphone and rant podcasts

The site **www.libsyn.com** boasts that its subscribers can simply "Grab a mic, get on your soapbox and let us take it from there". 'Libsyn' stands for Liberated Syndication. Again they'll deal with the RSS feeds and uploading your show onto the website.

Similarly, **www.podomatic.com** claims to be a "one stop shop for everything a podcaster would require".

With **www.audioblog.com** and **www.audioacrobat.com** you can phone your radio show in. You don't even need to buy a microphone!!

Reach for the stars

If you're podcasting on blog sites then gradually the most talented and entertaining broadcasters will shine through and become stars, building their own community of ardent listeners as word spreads.

It might be better for you to start your podcasting career this way – when you've built up your listenership and reputation, you could then buy your own website domain and build a bigger radio station.

Slowly you can become more independent, build on your knowledge and equipment and begin to turn your hobby into a lucrative business.

Remember

There are many blog sites that will publish your radio show without you getting involved in the more technical aspects of podcasting. They are a short cut for the budding podcast giant – but they do a wonderful job of getting your work heard by the world. Blog sites provide 'Quick Fix' podcasting.

A glimpse into the future

Now, blog site users (or bloggers) have started to video their messages on websites such as **www.youtube.com**.

Vodcasting (Video on Demand) is just as exciting as podcasting, but it's a little more difficult to distribute a vodcast – or to watch one on the go. For now, podcasts are still the most perfect medium for modern day entertainment.

"Every day, listeners from around the world are welcoming new broadcasters into their lives with open arms."

chapter 5
Radio paradise

Let's just to re-cap on what we've learned so far. To create a podcast there are two stages:

Stage one

1. Get a computer, microphone and website.
2. Download a computer programme, like Audacity, to record and edit your voice.
3. Have fun recording your radio show.
4. Convert your radio show into an MP3 file and upload it to your website, this might need a special File Transfer Programme (FTP).

Stage two

Either ...

1. Post your radio show onto your website – and tell your friends to listen!

Alternatively ...

2. Start getting serious. Create an RSS feed for your broadcast and inform as many aggregators as you wish that your radio show is now available for download to anyone who wants to listen all over the world. Aggregators will promote your show on their directories and distribute it for you. They'll also catch your new shows so that listeners who've subscribed will be automatically updated.

The quick fix option

A final option is the podcast short cut – ideal for the broadcaster who wants just a quick dabble in the broadcast revolution.

1. Go to one of the many blog sites – they'll give you your webpage, feed, and all you need to create your own show … You don't need a website or even a computer programme and all of the technical hard work is done for you.
2. No RSS forms or uploading here – all you'll have to do is talk!

Be amazed

Whichever route you choose, watch in delight as slowly the world begins listening to you, relating to you … reacting and interacting with you. Be amazed as slowly you pick up more and more listeners.

Finally, DON'T STOP PODCASTING. You're gradually becoming a radio star!

Talk, talk!

There are many superb website forums on podcasting. I've selected a few for you to check out. Their tutorials are well written, witty. and informative. Some of them also act as podcasting hosting sites and aggregators. The following sites talk podcasting in friendly terms, without the geek speak. They include …

www.radio.about.com, www.podcastalley.com, www.podcastpickle.com, www.podcast411.com, www.podcastingnews.com, www.how-to-podcast.com.

That should keep you going for a while … but there are plenty of others.

A golden nugget

While we are on the subject of radio paradise, how's this for podcasting's latest – and possibly greatest – innovation.

It's called Podscope – and can be found at **www.podscope.com**. Podscope is the first ever search engine developed specifically for hunting out the podcast of your dreams. It's a sort of Google for the podcasting world. Just enter a few key words describing the type of radio show you want to listen to - and Podscope does the rest.

The service hunts through the "podcast-o-sphere" and gives you a selection of shows that you might be interested in. You can play the whole show or just the snippet that contains your key words. If you like what you hear, you can subscribe. Podscope, invented by a company called TVEyes, is another huge leap forward for the podcasting phenomenon, which is very quickly transforming itself from mayhem to mainstream.

From fad ... to fab!

Remember

It's always a joy to tune in and listen to inspirational speakers.

But now, there's no need to use the phrase 'tune in' any more. It's old fashioned and relates to conventional radio. You don't 'tune in' to find podcasts ... they automatically find you!

The term 'tune in' will, in time, become consigned to the broadcasters' recycling bin!

chapter 6
Can you hear me, mother?

So, you don't think you've got the talent to cut it in the broadcasting world? Don't worry; you're about to surprise yourself! Creating your radio show and getting your message across effectively is much easier than it sounds. Once you've started broadcasting, you'll soon be hooked. Podcasting is a great medium of self-expression – and it's your great opportunity.

Have fun

Above anything else, the beauty of podcasting is that it's great fun. It can open the doors for you in so many different ways. It could lead you to new, vibrant social circles. You don't have to make a penny – podcasting can enrich your life in so many different ways.

If you only ever make one podcast in your life – it's still an achievement. Well done.

Big Brother is watching

Every single day, the world's top entertainment head hunters are listening to the world's podcast-o-sphere. They painstakingly trawl through the latest batch of shows to make sure they don't miss the next big thing.

In the words of one American media group: "We're keeping a close eye on edgy formats and radical ideas. Because listeners are making their own choices and not being forced to listen, it's clear to see who and what is successful."

Your first golden rules

1. **Always broadcast with passion**.
   You might have the most important message in the world ever! If it's not delivered with passion and a certain amount of authority then your message will not be heard.

2. **Claim your listeners**.
   They are part of your extended family now. Connect with them. Make them want to hear more. NEVER sound dull or uninterested – remember you have the most important message in the world to deliver.

3. **Accents don't count – in fact they can enhance your personality**.
   Use your accent to help create your own individual identity. Be yourself – don't try to sound like you think a professional broadcaster should sound.

4. **DON'T TRY TO BE COOL**.
   Be anything but cool. Be one of the family – your new extended family. Be angry, be funny, be strange – be very strange – but don't try to be cool!

5. **Personality wins listeners**.
   Use your personality to get your message across. Try to stand out from the crowd.

6. **Quality, Quality, Quality**.
   Your podcast must be as good – if not better – than anything else you can hear on conventional radio.

7. **Slow down and relax!**

The world's your oyster

You can record a podcast on literally any subject you like. If you've got something to say ... why not say it to the whole world?

You can use your newly acquired skills as an enjoyable and fulfilling hobby – or you can 'kick on' and turn that fulfilling hobby into a potentially lucrative career.

The more professional you sound – the more successful you'll be as a podcast pioneer.

One thing is for certain. Your show will evolve over time. You'll become more relaxed, you'll get to know your listener and you'll become a little more daring in your approach.

For now, here's how to become a great broadcaster in one easy chapter – you can go through years of training, but if you don't come across as a natural orator, then you'll never make a good broadcaster.

Remember

If you can broadcast with passion, yet sound relaxed; if you can project an air of authority, yet still come across as one of the family; if you can be unpredictable, yet stay confident ... you've cracked it.

You're well on the way to becoming a very successful professional broadcaster.

Your long-awaited debut

If you've never made a broadcast before, make sure you know what you want to say, and why you want to say it. Know exactly what your message is.

Don't be afraid to write down a few bullet points to help you along the way ... and always bring your broadcast to a conclusion – ask yourself "What's my punch line?" or "What's the main point of this broadcast – what am I trying to say?"

First impressions

The first 30 seconds of your broadcast are the most important.

Have you ever been to a bookshop and browsed at the blurb on the back cover of a book – the bit that tells you what the publication is about. Publishers reckon they've got less than a minute to impress readers with their front cover and blurb.

Listeners, like readers, make up their minds about a radio show in seconds.

Aggregators like iTunes give a small 'taster' for their radio shows, therefore it's vital that the beginning of your show is original enough to have listeners hooked straight away. Always hit the ground running.

One podcast I heard recently began with the words "Oops, sorry. I've dropped the microphone!" Whilst I found that quite amusing, it didn't encourage me to listen any further. I was gone in FOUR SECONDS. Listener lost – radio show doomed!

The big climax

The end of your show is just as important. Don't finish with a fluff – don't go out with a whimper. Finish with a flourish and go out with a bang. It encourages your listener to spread the word ... and look out for your next thrilling instalment.

First impressions and lasting impressions – they are both extremely important.

Creating a structure

So, we've started – and we've finished. What comes in between?

Although I would advise against a fully scripted radio show, it's always best to pen a simple structure or running order.

You need a basic outline of your show. Just a few pointers or sub-headings, so that, as a broadcaster, you've got some direction ... and you always know what's coming next.

See your running order as scaffolding around which to build your broadcast.

You could start with some introduction music followed by your welcome. A taster for what's coming up in the show, your first item, second item, third item. Your goodbye and 'outro' music. Easy as that.

Decide if you are going to broadcast solo or if you'll be using a co-host or guests.

A simple bit of planning makes you and your listener a little more comfortable. But don't be afraid to change it all around. Be spontaneous (you'll hear more about that soon!).

The outside broadcast

You don't have to stick to broadcasting from your newly created radio studio. You might want to get out and about and record some interviews at live venues or events to create an extra, sexy element to your radio show.

Don't be afraid to come out of the closet!

Occasionally the big names of sport, theatre, or television might be in town and you might get the chance to have five minutes to interview them – they won't come to your wardrobe to record the interview ... you'll have to go to them.

You can use almost any portable recording device such as a mini-disc, iRiver, Roland CD2, or MP3 recorder to capture an interview when you're out and about.

Then, simply transfer it onto your computer, and edit it later on.

Content is crucial

So ... what are you going to talk about? You need a 'hook' to hang your broadcast on. It's no good just babbling on for 15 minutes trying to sound interesting – that's a disaster. Unless you're a broadcasting master, you'll struggle to complete one broadcast, let alone a series.

Later on in this publication, we give you a multitude of hooks to hang your broadcast on. But if you've got a hobby or a particular interest that you want to tell others about (and pass on your hints and tips) that's always a good start.

Ask yourself again "What interests you? What are you passionate about?" You could have just given yourself the answer as to the content of your shows.

The niche market

Podcasting is excellent for reaching small, specific areas of interest – the niche market.

If you create your own niche market, then suddenly your broadcast will become a powerful source of information and enjoyment for those who share the same interest.

Your 'NicheCast' could very quickly turn you into an extremely wealthy and influential broadcaster / author / authority.

Remember

Podcasting has no rules. You can podcast on literally anything. You can sneeze into the microphone once a week if you like, though I can't guarantee you'll get a massive audience.

Using music in your show

Music is a great way to drive your show forward. It's nice to have a theme tune so listeners can identify with the show.

Using music also provides audio punctuation. A short blast (sting) represents a full stop. It makes for a smooth transition between segments of your show. Music keeps your show moving, it cues listeners into what's coming next.

Similarly, you can use music as a comfortable background to open and close your broadcast. Low volume music acts as a 'bed' for you to talk over which can be really effective. It also gives the broadcaster a safety net. If you lose your train of thought or need a moment's thinking space, simply turn your bed up and take a split second to compose yourself.

However, if you plan to use music in your programme that is not your own, you need to get permission. It's **not legal** to use copyright music in your podcast without permission.

Always follow my golden rule ... "If in doubt, leave it out."

Know your listener

It's vital that you know who you are aiming your broadcast at ... and then tailor both the length of your broadcast, and its content, to suit your listener.

Remember

'If you make it plain that you're interested in people, it's difficult for them to resist you in return. ' ... Another golden broadcasting tip for you – write it down and keep it by your microphone at all times.

The musical minefield

1. If it's not your music or if you don't have permission from the creators or owners of the music then don't use it.

2. Podsafe music is a rapidly growing area of the podcast world. If you're a Mac user on Garageband, you'll immediately be able to tap into a source of podsafe music. Have a rummage around for other podsafe music sources; **www.podcasterstingers.com** is just one website that allows podcasters to download and use stings and introduction music free of charge.

3. Royalty free music is another option. This is where you pay one fee which gives you the right to use the music whenever you like without paying more royalties.

4. Public domain. If music is considered to be in the public domain then you're probably free to use it. But again, always be careful or you might risk legal problems.

5. Do it yourself. Here's the safest bet. Have fun creating your own, original theme tunes and jingles, or get budding musicians to have a dabble for you. It's great experience and exposure for them and it's free and unique for you. Get creative. Produce your own identity and your own sound for your own unique radio brand.

Remember

Stay legal. If you are tempted to add music or sound effects to your radio broadcast, always make sure they are not copyright-protected. If in doubt … leave it out!

How long should my show be?

As long as it needs to be! You are in total control. Broadcasters are no longer limited to the ancient ways of radio timing. You don't have to talk up to the next news bulletin on the hour. You can be as flexible as you like.

If, during your show, you feel that you've got nothing else to say – then don't say it! If you feel you're brimming with extra information – save it for another time; tease your listener at the end of the programme with a couple of golden nuggets. Hint at what they can expect in the next scintillating episode. Whatever you do ... always leave your listeners begging for more.

The length of your broadcast depends on the type of show you are doing. But, as a general rule of thumb, try to make every programme around 20 minutes, or even less. In my personal opinion "only a fool breaks the 15 minute rule!"

Striking the balance

It's no good bombarding a listener with more radio shows than they can possibly handle. Go for a maximum of one every week. Fortnightly or monthly programmes are fine. At first, you'll struggle to maintain a daily podcast – and, believe it or not, your listeners might not want to hear you every day.

Remember

The big climax! Leave your listener wanting more so that it's a joy when the next shows lands into their laps and onto their ears. You've got them – don't lose them!

And don't talk about podcasting!

I know. You've been hooked by the podcasting bug and find it an exciting new phenomenon. You want to tell the world about it.

Don't!

Use podcasting to create new, enthralling, groundbreaking radio shows. Podcasting is ONLY your 'talent tool'. Use it to take your talent to the world. It's your blank canvas on which to paint your new life. Remember, podcasting is for passionate, talented broadcasters – not for techno-bores!

Watch your step!

Because Podcasting is still in its infancy, there is currently no regulatory system in place. Always be aware of what you are broadcasting and who you are broadcasting to. This publication does not condone, in any form, the use of bad language, poor taste, or subjects likely to offend in any of its podcasts.

Keep it entertaining but also keep it tasteful – and keep it clean!

Size doesn't matter

As we've just covered the subject of decency, it's worth remembering that size is not important!

Getting your message across has little to do with the amount of money you spend on creating your radio station, and being a successful broadcaster has nothing to do with the size, or cost, of your kit.

In the words of the great inventor Thomas A Edison (1847-1931): "To invent you simply need a good imagination and a pile of junk!"

"Your time has come … if you've got something to say, say it to the world.

Protecting your work

So, you're unique. You're witty. You're creative. You're a genius. But you don't want other people stealing your ideas and hard work.

So, can you copyright your podcast?

The answer is yes ... and guess what ... it's simple, and free.

The non-profit making organisation **www.creativecommons.org** is offering flexible copyright licences to the podcaster, totally free of charge. They boast "Everything we do, including the software we create, is free".

Setting out your stall

Although this next golden nugget of advice sounds obvious, it's vitally important:

The world's most successful broadcasters are the ones most liked (or disliked) by the listeners. It's better for a listener to have an opinion about you either way – than not to care at all.

If you're setting out to be controversial in your broadcasts, fine! Go for broke. Make the listeners disagree passionately with you – but don't let them ignore you. Set out your stall, create a valid argument and put your point across. Invite your listener to disagree with you – spark comment and debate with your listener, however much they disagree, they'll come back for more. When you're more established, it's easy to create a phone-in element to your podcasts. Don't be afraid to use it – it could be the making of you.

If you're setting out to be friendly, fine! Make yourself one of the family. Become a presenter that the listener can relate to and be friends with. Make them laugh with you – even sympathise and cry with you.

A unique partnership

Never separate yourself from the listener. To be a successful broadcaster you must take your listener on every step of your exciting journey. It's a two-way thing ... a unique partnership. One can't operate without the other, and interaction between the listener and the broadcaster is always essential. Try to connect with the listener at all times.

Always mention the names of people who correspond with you. Listeners love hearing their names mentioned, it adds the personal touch. They suddenly feel like one of your "team". Encourage others to do the same and NEVER be afraid to let your listener lead the way. Ask them what they want to hear.

The perfect face for radio!

It's radio. Nobody can see you!! Have a few tries. Your first podcast doesn't have to go out – these are not live radio shows.

Experiment. Have a listen to other podcasts – see what's already out there, and learn from the best ones. (There are a few excellent broadcasters in the podcast-o-sphere ... but an awful lot of rubbish. I'm sure you can do a lot better than most.)

Practice makes perfect, although – in broadcasting – there's nothing wrong with being a little rough around the edges ... as long as you connect with your listener.

Never make it sound as though you're reading from a script. Make your broadcast as natural as possible. Enjoy yourself. If you've got a fun message, then broadcast it with a smile on your face!

Listeners can tell a great deal about you – not from what you're saying, but how you're saying it. They'll build up a mental picture of what you look like. They'll know whether you are uptight or nervous just by how you're putting your message across. Try to be relaxed, natural and confident. Take control of the airwaves and never stop being your listeners' best buddy.

If in doubt, tell them you look like Brad Pitt!

The performance zone

Yes, sometimes it might be your job, as the world's newest broadcaster, to inform. But more importantly it's your job to entertain.

Whatever your broadcast subject, MAKE IT A PERFORMANCE. Keep in that performance zone throughout the duration of your radio show. Be relaxed at all times, but have the listener hanging on to your every word.

Becoming a cult

If your podcast becomes cult listening then you're onto a massive winner. Word of mouth will spread and everyone will want to get involved.

Cult podcasts will attract huge worldwide audiences... and huge worldwide audiences will attract both massive sponsorship and pay-per-listen subscription – the ultimate podcaster's paradise. (You'll learn more about that later.)

For now, here's one pleasant thought ... cult listening could easily turn you into a wealthy and famous broadcaster. You'll be making money doing the thing you enjoy most – what could be better or more satisfying?

Who said you'll never be a radio star?

Virtually all radio stars of the future will emerge from the ranks of my new podcast pioneers. But always be yourself – use your personality. Don't try to sound like a radio broadcaster – you're unique.

We don't need to hear another robot on the radio – we've heard them all before. We need to hear you. We've never heard you broadcast before ... and you're a one-off.

Keep them guessing

"I don't know what you're going to come out with next!" is one of the finest compliments a listener can pay to a broadcaster. As we've already mentioned, don't be afraid to be spontaneous and unpredictable, yet always remain in control and know where your broadcast is heading.

Imagine for a moment that I'm your listener. I've chosen to listen to your broadcast because you're talking about a subject I'm interested in. That's the beauty of podcasting. I've chosen to listen to your show because it sounds as if I might be stimulated by it. Congratulations, you've got a listener. You're halfway there.

You've got me - don't lose me. MAKE ME STICK WITH YOU! Make it so that I can't afford to switch off or stop my subscription. Engage me in your debate, embrace me with your warm personality – speak to me and only me. Make me a part of your world and don't let me lose interest at any time.

Make me your best friend.

Take me on a magical mystery trip every show.

Talk to me like you would talk to your mates in the pub.

Amuse me; infuriate me; intrigue me; anger me; delight and surprise me...

BUT DON'T LOSE ME!

Remember

You are at the cutting, thrusting edge of a new broadcasting era and you've got the most important message in the world. Demand your listeners' full attention at all times. Your radio style and format will grow, along with your listeners, over a period of time. Let it evolve – and grow with it. Now who says you'll never be a radio star?

chapter 7
Creating your empire

So, you fancy broadcasting to the world, do you? Ideally, you'd love to turn your new hobby into a full time, lucrative business.

Can it be done? Of course ...

Your route to podcasting prosperity

When you've become comfortable with the technical side of things, and you've mastered the art of 'putting your message across', you can begin gradually upgrading and developing your equipment until you've built yourself a small, yet highly adequate broadcasting studio.

Then, together with the tips in this book, you'll be in a position to start turning your new passion into a lucrative business.

But I'm still a virgin!

It doesn't really matter if you're an established broadcaster or a broadcast virgin. The message is the same ... hold on tight. I'm about to inspire you.

You'll see how exciting the podcast world can be for you. What massive, but so far undiscovered, opportunities are out there for the new generation of broadcast heroes and heroines?

At long last, we're going to throw the doors wide open, so that a whole new generation of capable communicators can finally make their mark on the broadcasting universe.

Making money from your podcasts

There are three ways to make money from your podcast empire.

1. Create a show that advertises a specific product or service. Businesses will be willing to pay for your broadcasting services because these podcasts will get their message direct to the people they want to target (their customers), wherever they are in the world – at the touch of a button.

   We're about to delve deeper into this option, using Podverts and PodFlashes – two new, fun concepts that will revolutionise the broadcasting, advertising, and business world.

2. Make a star of yourself. Create a show that people will pay to subscribe to. If you can build up a base of fans who are prepared to pay a small amount of money to listen to your talents, that will soon grow into potentially lucrative pickings.

   As I mentioned in the previous chapter, if your radio show attracts cult listening, then you're onto a potential goldmine. 'Pay-per-listen' shows could make you a very wealthy broadcaster.

3. Carry adverts or have your shows sponsored. You're the boss. It's your radio station – you can carry advertisements if you like; it's up to you.

   In some ways, this goes hand-in-hand with our second option. Successful shows will attract large numbers of listeners. The bigger your audience, the easier it will be to persuade advertisers and sponsors to back your broadcast and send their message to your fans.

Podcasting paradise

The ultimate goal for any podcaster is to combine the options outlined above. Creating a radio show that is entertaining enough for people to pay to listen to – and is attractive enough for businesses to advertise on. If you can achieve those two aims – you will become a very successful, and very wealthy broadcaster. I absolutely 100 per cent guarantee it!

Be a quality podcast producer

Believe it or not, you don't have to be a clever broadcaster to make money through podcasting. In fact, you don't have to broadcast at all!

If you're more turned on by the technicals, you can easily build a thriving business by producing or helping to produce quality broadcasts for companies, groups, or individuals, whatever their specific needs and interests. As podcasting grows and grows, your new studio could be hired out by hundreds of new broadcasters eager to claim their slice of radio heaven – and just as desperate for a bit of advice along the way.

Making good 'Ad' sense

Of course, another crucial way to make money through podcasting is to attract advertising on your website or blog. Have a look at 'Google Adsense' it's one way you can achieve this aim.

Adsense automatically crawls through the content of your WebPages and places adverts on them that may be relevant or useful to your visitors. When someone clicks the ads, you get paid a fee. Simple!

Money, money, money

Of course, listeners probably won't want to pay to hear your shows in the beginning – especially if you're relatively unknown in the broadcasting world. Unless you're a niche podcaster, you'll probably have to build a reputation and audience base first.

When you've started to construct a healthy fan base, why not get creative with the way people pay to listen to you. For example, if you base your podcast on a pub conversation, create your imaginary pub and ask your audience to "buy you a drink"! That way you can give the listener a name check (and drink to his or her health).

I guarantee that your listeners will be happy to pitch in and hear their names read out as you raise a glass to them. They'll be paying to listen to your show without even realising it. Remember, as we've already said – podcasting is a two-way partnership between you and the listener. The more creative you can get with your pay-per-listen ideas, the more successful you'll be.

Laying down the gauntlet

Your time has come. I want to create hundreds of new podcast pioneers, presenters, and entrepreneurs. It's time to take the world of the podcast on to a new level, smashing through the boundaries to discover that vibrant, unclaimed territory we spoke of at the very start of the book. It's time to lay down the gauntlet to the world of the established broadcaster.

Remember

Unless you attempt to do something beyond what you have already mastered, you will never grow.

"The broadcasting world is watching you. Original ideas and edgy formats will create radio's biggest stars of the future.

chapter 8
The glorious world of the podvert

Let's investigate the first option for making money from your new broadcasting career. We're about to use podcasting to shake up the business world.

What the hell's a Podvert?!

It's an advert, delivered direct to a customer or potential customer in the form of a podcast. Companies can now reach their prospective punters direct – wherever they are in the world – at a fraction of the cost of conventional advertising on radio, television, or in newspapers. A Podvert is far more impressive than a conventional advert. Firstly, it goes instantly around the world. It gives a company, however big or small, the chance to advertise its product or service direct to the customer. It's their chance to talk, one-to-one, ear-to-ear, and almost face-to-face with a prospective punter on a global stage.

A Podvert hits prospective punters right between the ears!

It's happening!

Two thirds of senior executives in the media and entertainment industry believe that within three years, podcast pioneers will be making substantial financial gains through advertising and sponsorship of their social media.

But how can I make Podverts work for me?

There are many different ways that you, the podcast pioneer, can cash in on the impending Podvert boom. You can set yourself up as a Podvert producer, helping businesses create the perfect broadcast on which to promote their product, service, or entertainment venue.

You can advise company spokesmen and women on how they can transform themselves into professional presenters to help get the message across. You can present the Podvert yourself, or even get a celebrity to present it, depending on the size of the company or the budget. There are a variety of riveting ways in which you can help companies with their Podvert. They'll love the idea – they'll think it sexy, new, and innovative.

Let's get creative

But who will want to listen to a boring old advert?

I'm about to open your minds to a number of so far undiscovered devices to turn the Podvert into an entertaining experience for any listener. The Podvert can take many forms. If a company has a new, innovating product to sell, then of course people will want to hear about it. The more wacky, unique, or inventive the product, the more people will want to know about it. A whole broadcast or series of high quality radio shows can be produced and made available, free of charge, to subscribers worldwide to let them know about the new product or service and how it could change their lives.

Imagine that …

You can help company chiefs spread the word about their new product or service all around the world for a fraction of the cost of conventional advertising. What's more, they'll be talking DIRECT to the people who are most likely to want to purchase the product.

Virtually all companies have a website – the ideal launching pad for airing their new radio show. At the click of a "listen here" chicklet on the webpage, their business message could fly instantly around the world. Congratulations, their company is now an active player in our radio revolution!

Let's take this up a level and raise the bar

If their company's product is not unique enough to stand alone as the star of its own podcast … then we'll disguise it. We'll build an exciting radio show around the product to show it off, indirectly to the listeners. It that way, listeners will be enjoying their radio show, and won't realise that they are listening to an advert.

Let's start with a modest example and work our way up to our ultimate 'take over the planet' device. If you read on, we'll give you the capability and encouragement to change the face of advertising for good, through the new world of the podcast.

Remember

Start small and work your way up. Target a batch of local companies and introduce them to the breathtaking world of the podcast. Then tell them how you can help get their message to the world, at a fraction of the cost of conventional television, radio, or newspaper advertisements.

Going down the PodPan!

The PodPan Indian Restaurant is about to open its doors in trendy CastVille. Why not offer to produce, for our hardworking friends at the PodPan Indian Restaurant, their own cookery radio show? The chefs could take centre stage, guiding listeners through the delights of fine Indian cuisine in an entertaining and informative way. Who knows, you might be inadvertently creating a future superstar chef.

As well as creating an entertaining and informing podcast, you mention that the dishes are always available from the PodPan Indian Restaurant. You can also use the "This podcast was brought to you by ... " approach throughout the show, although be careful that your advertising is not too rampant or else the value and quality of your podcast could be undermined.

Get it out there

Once your PodPan Podvert has been recorded, make it available on the restaurant's website. You can also get it sent out to the world via one of the many aggregators. Soon everyone will be latching on to this "entertaining new Indian cookery show – on podcast". That means every listener will also know about the PodPan Indian Restaurant. Your message has been spread around the world in an instant. Furthermore, fans of Indian food – those most likely to want to use the restaurant – are hearing it.

Now we're beginning to fly

Once you've created one Podvert you can put together a series of proposals to many other firms or businesses. Create your own Podvert stable. Your reputation as a quality podcaster will soon begin to grow and word will spread – companies might even start hunting you out.

Remember

Companies are only just beginning to wake up to the podcast revolution. Presenting your idea will be just as exciting for them. Tell them how they'll be at the forefront of a new broadcasting era, namely Radio on Demand. Explain what an exciting, new, and relatively untapped medium they now have for promoting their business.

Now let's change the world

It's time to investigate some really breathtaking ways in which the Podvert can transform the world of broadcasting.

A Podvert goldmine – part one

How much do the multi-national sportswear firms spend on advertising each year?

Now they can reach their target audience, wherever they live around the globe, at the touch of a button.

Here's the plan – it'll make my fantasy sportswear company millions of pounds, save them a fortune, and enhance their name with the spin-off of endless, free global publicity.

Imagine my firm has signed up a mega football star to wear its new boots. As part of the deal, the footballer could be featured in a series of podcasts to help youngsters worldwide improve their soccer skills.

Imagine that …

It's a kid's dream. A ten-minute monthly football lesson from their favourite player! Delivered direct to them, free of charge.

A football-mad child can receive his or her own personal soccer lesson – from their ultimate hero – direct to his or her iPod or MP3 player, or download it at the click of a button from the company website. The flood of international publicity on the launch would be immense – and the thrill for the youngsters would be enormous.

The football megastar is helping to breed a whole new nation of football superstars – and he's spreading the message of his sportswear firm in the most entertaining and revolutionary fashion.

GOOOOOAAAAALLLLLLLL!

A Podvert goldmine – part two

Cash in on the Podvert boom by creating programmes that will have companies clamouring to place their product on your show.

Create the programme first, and then go to your targeted company to see how quickly they jump on board. I'm sure you'll be pleasantly surprised.

Remember

In the words of Michael Geohegan, chief executive of GigaVox Media: "At the moment, too many podcasters undervalue the asset they are building and end up not achieving the financial returns they deserve."

The greatest podcast in the world!

Using my publisher's trademarked brand as an example, no green-fingered enthusiast in their right mind could resist a show entitled The Greatest Gardening Tips in the World. What a fantastic podcast for a gardening firm or garden centre to put its name to.

The Greatest Tips in the World series of broadcasts can be adapted (and adopted) as a Podvert by almost any company you like. The Greatest Household Tips / The Greatest DIY Tips / The Greatest Fishing Tips ... the list and the possibilities are endless.

Present the idea to your targeted company and ask them to sponsor it with their own advertisement or acknowledgement ("brought to you by ..."). Alternatively, they can get their products mentioned as part of the greatest tips. For example: "It's always best to use a quality spade – I wouldn't be without my ..."

Take it and run with it

Similarly, garden centres can lend their name to an ask-the-experts Podvert. Their websites can be used in conjunction with the podcast. Not only can people download the programme direct from the company website, they can also leave their questions for the experts to answer. The same approach could be used for a Do-It-Yourself store.

If you're creating a Podvert based on cookery, gardening, DIY or the like, always remember the value of using a local, national, or even international celebrity to front the broadcast – the celebrity doesn't even have to be an expert in the field – just a well known, well-liked (or even a well-hated) figure who is going to make people take note, download the show... and listen. You'll read more about the beauty of celebrity podcasts later on.

Podverts, Podverts everywhere

When you start to think about it, there are hundreds of ways in which your broadcast could be adapted to sell a company's product or service.

Have fun and get creative! Who could resist a show entitled "The greatest / most unusual Christmas gifts ever". Put out your proposal to dozens of companies. Get them in on the act and charge them for placing their product on your podcast.

It's a two-way thing. You're creating a quality, informative and entertaining podcast for the listener as well as a hugely valuable advertising outlet for companies wishing to place their product and invest in your revolutionary new broadcast empire.

How about "Top tips on cleaning your house" – sponsored by a detergent company? Or "How to look ten years younger by simply changing your outfit" sponsored by, you've guessed it, a clothing brand!

Slinging the schedules

Because listeners are no longer burdened by schedules, niche podcasters will start to flourish like never before.

Sometimes the more wacky or specialist the Podvert – the more successful it will be. For example: 'How to keep chickens' sponsored by a chicken food or coup building firm or 'How to dress your ferrets' backed by a ferret-clothing outlet. Where there's a hobby, there will almost certainly be a company behind it providing goods and services to the enthusiast concerned.

You can't fail

If you chose to produce and present this form of podcast, you too could very easily stumble into the limelight (as many established stars have already done on antiques, cookery, house and gardening shows). What better way to thrust yourself on an unsuspecting public and launch your own successful career than as a presenter of this type of broadcast? It's a great platform on which to launch a media career of your own.

And you'll be making money while you gather your own little fan base.

It's all out there on a plate

The goldmine ideas are just a small taste of how the Podvert can work for almost any business or company. Digest the concept and then develop it to complement your individual tastes, style, or talents. As my podcast pioneer, you could professionally produce the Podvert broadcasts. Make them of the highest quality possible. Start with small companies and then build up.

Create a Podvert stable – your own little empire. Tap into your own niche market (as we mentioned earlier on) and go for broke. Before long, you could have an extremely profitable business on your hands.

Remember

Whatever your podcast idea, pen your proposal carefully. Use some of the facts and advice contained in this book. That's what it's for. Why not produce a dummy podcast so your clients can get a feel for what this new business is all about – and how much of a revelation it will be for them.

chapter 9

Spreading the word – in a flash!

Is it a bird? Is it a plane? No … !

Ladies and gentlemen, the PodFlash has landed. This is one of the jewels in my podcasting crown. It encompasses everything you've learnt so far and can be used in a variety of creative, not to mention lucrative, ways.

So far we've concentrated on a fully blown radio programme (don't forget, it should be no more than 20 minutes long). The PodFlash is something completely different. This is a bright, bold and breezy radio jingle (or 'Pingle' if your prefer!) that is no more than **two minutes** in length. Stunningly simple, yet blissfully effective. The PodFlash is so small that it can be used by companies that already have a list of the email addresses of their established customers.

How does it work?

So far we've talked about potential listeners downloading radio shows directly. We've steered clear of companies sending out regular 15 minute radio shows to their own mailing list clients, by email attachment. Some folks might not want to receive them, others might be concerned about the download time of such shows blocking up their computer tubes! The odd few may not be ready to join our revolution yet.

The PodFlash, however, is unique. It it can be downloaded in seconds and, if it's a minute long, it takes a minute to listen to!

It's believed that podcasting will evolve into the most serious challenge to conventional radio since the advent of television.

So who can use a PodFlash?

Everyone and anyone. If a business, say your local theatre, wants to alert customers on their current mailing list to a new show or breaking news of a star who's coming to town, they simply send – via email attachment to each and every member of their mailing list (or even direct to a customer's mobile phone) – a PodFlash.

Take it and run with it

Maybe your sports club could use a PodFlash to keep fans bang up to date with new breaking transfer stories or ticket information. It's news as it happens. Radio on Demand.

Flash in the PodPan

Hotels and restaurants (remember our PodPan Indian eating house?) can alert their existing clientele about special offers and reduced accommodation rates. If they are already operating a full-scale podcast, the two can sit very nicely together – each one complementing the other. A PodFlash encouraging even more listeners to download the accompanying podcast.

Your in-house flash

Businesses could even use the PodFlash to complement their in-house information service. Rather than a boring email – why not inform your employees of the day's events on PodFlash? It's up-to-the-minute, breaking news in a podcast. A superb service for any company or venue... and it's at the cutting, thrusting edge of a broadcasting revolution.

It's a beauty

A PodFlash can be sent, by attachment, to the email addresses of all your existing customers. A PodFlash downloads in a flash, literally, and it's a delight to listen to – what a refreshing change to a boring old pamphlet through the post.

Has there ever been a more direct and exciting way to reach your potential clients? Don't send a letter to your customers and potential punters – send them a PodFlash to listen to.

Of course, once you've sold the idea of producing and/or voicing the PodFlash to a client such as an amusement park, you might then want to introduce them to a full scale podcast – their own radio show on their own radio station.

Sex it up!

Base your PodFlash on the conventional radio advert. Make it bright and bold. Demand your listeners' attention at all times. Have a distinctive music bed so that your PodFlash becomes instantly recognisable. Don't be afraid to add a second voice or as many sound bites as you can comfortably fit in to ram your message home.

Little things mean a lot

In the case of the PodFlash, small is definitely beautiful …
but if you create a stable or small empire of companies who want you to produce their quality PodFlash – the small package could result in rather large earnings.

You could be earning a fortune … in a flash.

Or even a PodFlash!

Your arch enemy!

As we've already discussed, podcasting is evolving almost every second – that's what makes it so enthralling.

But beware! There are a few bad guys in the ranks, lobbing barriers in the path of the pioneers. One such villain is known as ... 'Audience Measurement' the podcasters' sworn enemy.

Although podcasters can identify how many times their show has been downloaded, they can't currently measure how many times it's actually been listened to. Until such measurements are in place many traditional radio advertisers are treating the impending podcast boom with caution ... and that's bad news.

Of course, this enemy will be soundly defeated in time. Very soon, a device that can accurately measure a podcast audience will be concocted ... and advertisers will be flocking to peddle their wears on your shows.

Let the audience measurement battle commence!

chapter 10
A hook to hang your broadcast on

Podverts and PodFlashes are two exciting ways in which you can make money by sharing your new podcasting talent with the business world.

Now let's return to the notion of making a radio show that could potentially turn you into a broadcasting star.

The dream scene

The next range of working models is based on the dream scenario of creating a successful radio show that will attract pay-per-listen subscription and sponsorship. Remember, at the start of the book we asked "What shall I talk about?" We mentioned that content is crucial to a successful radio broadcast.

Well, here are some inspirational ideas, or hooks, to hang your broadcast on.

It's not an exhaustive list — that's something that will continue to grow and grow as the next few years pass by.

Remember

The following examples are working models, but their formats can be applied to almost any type of podcast.

Have fun!

And don't forget ... there are no boundaries and no limits.

The SportsCast…

Frankly, sports fans, this idea is a potential money-making dream for the sports minded. This is my FA Cup of podcasts. No, I'll go one better – we're in the UEFA Champions League now. If you're reading this publication in America, this is the Superbowl of ideas. Indeed, the plan is appropriate for every sport: baseball, American football, sumo wrestling, cricket, rugby, Aussie rules, conkers or wife carrying!

A sporting paradise

Sports fanatics, wherever they are in the world, feed on information from their clubs. They devour every last snippet. They talk about every small detail at great length in their pubs and social clubs. Their club is their religion and they eat, drink, and sleep it.

A league apart

How fantastic, then, to have a weekly radio show delivered directly to supporters, focussing solely on their favourite sports club. No more will they have to sit through hours of radio phone-ins waiting for their team to be mentioned.

No more will they scour the back pages of every newspaper looking for one lowly paragraph of information. The SportsCast is for sports fanatics, wherever they are in the world – it's their club, their radio show, their forum – and in some cases, their lifeline.

British football fans may remember Clubcall – a telephone information service that was extremely lucrative in the 1980s and 1990s. Football supporters would phone a high premium telephone number to get all the latest news and gossip from their clubs. Podcasting is about to take-off massively where "Clubcall" bit the dust.

Through the worldwide aggregators, fans and fanatics could subscribe (free of charge or at a small cost) to a SportsCast. That way, they would be guaranteed to receive the next thrilling instalment automatically ... so they wouldn't miss a kick (so to speak).

Planting the seed

Why not offer to produce a high quality, entertaining SportsCast for your chosen club? Put a proposal together for the team's bosses. The idea will be so interesting that they'll be sure to want to hear more.

Have all your facts ready and prepare to thrill your targeted club by taking them into a new world.

You could even put yourself forward as a presenter of the show. What a fantastic way to launch your sports broadcasting career.

Once you're producing a SportsCast for one club, you could easily go for a second. You'll have the experience and your reputation will be spreading. Gradually you'll be creating a SportsCast empire.

Remember

You don't need an ipod to listen to podcasts. There's an ever-growing list of podcast-friendly devices, which means you can hear your favourite show on the go ... even at the match.

These devices already include MP3 players, mobile phones, computers, sunglasses ... And even a pair of diving goggles!

Everyone's a winner, baby

If your SportsCast is free to subscribers, clubs can still make money whilst providing a groundbreaking new service for its long-suffering fans. They simply have to get their SportsCasts sponsored. The club's major backer would almost certainly be in a prime position to get involved with adverts on the podcast.

And don't forget the use of a PodFlash. All sports clubs have the email addresses of fans (their mailing list) and the PodFlash can keep those fans up-to-date with all breaking news (and ticket information) from a club ... in a flash!

The FanCast

There are many other ways of making a business through the SportsCast network. Fanzines have, for many years, helped feed the sports fan's ceaseless craving for information. These publications however, are now on the decline – podcast fanzines (or FanCasts) are set to replace them.

Professional sounding FanCasts can also be sponsored and would be free to subscribers. Remember, the more subscribers you get the more chance you've got of picking up extra sponsorship.

Create your FanCast so there's a forum for fans to chat / gossip / praise and criticise. Have a website where fans can leave their opinions. As with all podcasts, don't be afraid to add a phone-in element. Contact the fans and talk to them on the show.

Home and away

Fans who have now left the area could keep up to date on the goings-on at their beloved club, wherever they are in the world. It's their little slice of home – while they are away!

Creating a SportsCast goldmine

1. If your club has a celebrity fan, why not approach him or her about making a short monthly broadcast.

2. Remember, the bigger the celebrity, the bigger the audience and the higher the earning potential.

3. Podcaster Rovers, let's imagine, are supported by world-renowned rock star Johnny Fame. "Johnny Fame's Football World" – a monthly podcast by the man himself would create a huge amount of interest from football fans not just of the club, but also worldwide.

4. Former sports stars could also be fertile ground for a SportsCast. (Or in this case, a new series – The PodLegends!). PodLegends from all sports could air their views on the games and deliver their informed opinion direct to the fans. (You'll read more about PodLegends later on).

The grass roots

SportsCasts are not just limited to the glamorous teams and celebrity fans.

Even the most humble of sports teams has its loyal supporters... and more importantly, sponsors. Now their fans can get up-to-the-minute news and views on their beloved club by way of their very own SportsCast. The club could pay you to produce the SportsCast, but don't forget to tell them how they could cash in by having the broadcast sponsored.

Indeed, SportsCasting doesn't have to be restricted to a single team. A whole league could have its regular radio show. Sponsorship here could come from the league's main backers. And minority sports can have a SportsCast aimed at a whole sport, rather than just a club.

The EduCast...

If you have a specific talent and would like to share it with the world – then here's your chance. It's also your golden opportunity to make money through your skill or hobby.

Welcome to the new and exciting world of the "EduCast".

Clive's fortune

Clive Fortune is a top class musician. He appeared in a string of pop bands in the 1960s and achieved small-scale success with his self-penned classic "Pod, Pod the Caster Man" which flirted with the hit parade's top 50 in 1967.

Since he left the limelight, Clive has been working as a music teacher – his lessons have been limping along steadily for the last four decades... until now.

Clive could transform himself and his business in an instant by joining my podcast revolution. He could create a series of EduCasts, which would help students worldwide master the art of playing the guitar, drums, or the keyboards.

The former rock star could suddenly become an overnight podcast pioneer. For a small subscription fee, he could be teaching budding Buddy Holly's all over the world.

All they would need is a guitar and Clive's monthly podcast, which would automatically be downloaded direct to them and updated whenever they're ready to move onto the next stage. Clive's customers could be playing their chosen musical instrument within the blow of a trombone.

Podcasting is
a great medium
for self-expression
… and it's your
once in a lifetime
opportunity.

Making your name

Clive could soon develop a cult following with his quality, entertaining teach-ins. He would be enjoying the huge satisfaction of passing on his skills to an army of new students around the globe … and he could be pocketing a small fortune along the way. (Get it? Clive earning a small 'fortune'! Oh, never mind!)

And now he has become one of the world's first EduCast pioneers, Clive can use his monthly radio show to showcase himself. He could produce a book or E-book to accompany his lessons –he might even be able to re-release "Pod, Pod the Caster Man"! He could very easily attract sponsors and advertisers onto his show (musical instrument manufacturers, for example), increasing his revenue still further. And his students could conquer the art of playing many different musical instruments at all levels. The series could be never ending.

I'm a celebrity – get me in here!

If Clive Fortune can make a bob or two from his music, just imagine how popular lessons from an established rock star would be. And what fantastic publicity for the singer or musician concerned.

How much would you pay to have a personal guitar lesson with your idol? Now it could be possible.

How's this for starters … "Learning the piano with Johnny Fame". (Remember him? He's the celebrity Podcaster Rovers fan we met while putting together our SportsCasts.) Johnny's monthly piano podcasts would automatically be a worldwide best seller. They could well make Fame a fortune!

Imagine that…

It's radio heaven for the listeners. His or her own personal "lesson with a legend" delivered every month, direct to the student's own iPod or MP3 player. It sounds almost too good to be true – but it could happen – and very likely will in the not too distant future.

The subscription fees alone would certainly add to the star's already substantial earnings... but the publicity value of getting guitar lessons direct from Eric Clapton or learning the drums with Phil Collins. Can you imagine? It would be enough to get the national newspapers drooling (similar to the soccer star involved in our Podvert earlier on).

Remember

Celebrity podcasts are set to become a worldwide phenomenon. RadioHeaven.com is one of the podcast radio stations leading the way in this field. They have a range of featured celebrities from pop idol Donny Osmond to the legend of the silver screen, Sir Richard Attenborough.

RadioHeaven.com is a good example of a podcast station attempting to push back the boundaries to take podcasting to the next level.

Education, education, education

Of course, the EduCast series isn't just designed for learning a new instrument. It can be developed for teaching students a new language, learning to write or paint; even teaching budding radio stars how to broadcast – a radio course on the radio!

Harry Podder!

Talking books certainly fall under the "EduCast" umbrella.

All books can be turned into podcasts. They can be used by anybody. The partially sighted would, of course, benefit hugely from such a service. Many classics (and not so classics) could be turned into podcasts for anyone and everyone to enjoy, wherever they chose. Don't take a book on holiday – download one and listen to it at your leisure.

If you can get a celebrity to read your book and turn it into a podcast, you might get more subscribers still. It's Jackanory brought kicking and screaming into the technological age.

Your podcast teach-in

University and college tutors can now record their lectures on podcast. Ideal for part time students who want to enhance their qualifications, or gain new ones, from the comfort of their own living room, kitchen or car.

It's University for All ... wherever they are in the world.

Your EduCast famous five … !

Here are five more great tips for creating successful podcasts under the EduCast umbrella.

1 On the school run

Schools could use podcasting as an exciting new medium for their students. They could easily create their own school radio station, broadcasting shows to parents and pupils alike – either posted onto the school website or delivered automatically for parents and pupils to listen to on their portable players.

Complement the old-fashioned school letter with an up to-the-minute radio bulletin, produced and presented by the students themselves. What an exciting way to get students involved in broadcasting. And what a valuable tool for any English teachers.

You can even use a PodFlash to keep parents up-to-date … in a flash!

2 The TravelCast

Imagine you're about to travel to a holiday destination, or on a well-deserved mini break somewhere in the world. What a lovely treat if your travel agent, as well as providing the tickets and making the arrangements, suddenly delivered a free radio programme about the place you are going to visit, direct to your computer. What might be worth a visit on your arrival? What you simply can't afford to miss … and what to avoid at all costs.

Travel companies could benefit hugely from adding their name to the TravelCast. So could the destinations themselves – as I'm about to outline with another fun idea.

A BardCast a BardCast, my kingdom for a BardCast

Stratford-upon-Avon in the U.K. is a great example of a money-making podcast... in the making! Visitors from all over the world visit Stratford, which is globally famous for being the birthplace of a certain William Shakespeare.

Tourism chiefs in Stratford could cash in hugely by creating their own show... a "BardCast". An entertaining, yet informative, radio show telling people about the town's many Shakespeare attractions. How much it costs to get into the museums. What's on at the Royal Shakespeare Theatre and how to get tickets. Shakespeare himself could be the show's presenter! Imagine that. William Shakespeare ... the world's newest radio celebrity!

The town will enjoy a massive amount of publicity simply by launching the service, and tourist chiefs could even make money for the town by getting their BardCast sponsored by local hotels or restaurants. Almost any holiday destination or city could benefit enormously from its own version of a BardCast.

It's happening!

Vintage wireless shows are being reborn thanks to the growth in podcasting. Remarkably, some of the most popular stars of the On Demand boom, are names that were first discovered during the golden age of radio from the 1930s to the 1950s. Classic radio dramas like 'Sherlock Holmes' and 'Dick Barton – Special Agent' are proving to be popular. Who would have thought that 'The Lone Ranger' was one of the most popular podcast stars of 2005? His adventures from 1938 are now being discovered and rediscovered by listeners of all ages.

PupCasts

There's even room for non-humans in the EduCast camp.
A regular dog-training podcast, a PupCast could easily be a very
big hit with the canine crazy. Who's going to be the next Barbara
Woodhouse? A PupCast would be ideal for sponsorship from any
of the world's giant "pooch pampering" organisations.

Of course, it doesn't have to be dogs.

Pet tip podcasts are a potential goldmine. They have a ready
made audience — and potential sponsors who could be queuing
up to get their message direct to the people who most need their
goods and services.

The talking tour

Why not take the world of the "talking tour" to another level?
Many museums, art galleries and other attractions could provide
an audio service for their clients. They could create a talking tour
of their star attractions, historic sights and places or exhibits
of interest, via podcast, using a hired iPod or MP3 player.

They could jazz up the talking tour — making it original and
entertaining. Why not help drag your local museum or art
gallery into a new age of technology and give their visitors
an unexpected and rare treat?

Those are just five EduCast options... now let's discover some
other fun hooks to hang your radio shows on.

The StarCast …

Aries, Taurus, Gemini, Cancer, Leo, Virgo, Libra, Scorpio, Sagittarius, Capricorn, Aquarius, Pisces …

Here's one for the astrologists among us.

Reading a daily horoscope is a way of life for many people. For a good number of years, mystic fairs have been popular amongst those of us who wish to delve into the future to take a sneaky peek at what might be just around the corner.

Introducing Mrs Crystal Ball

Barbara "Crystal" Ball, our imaginary astrologer, has been studying the stars for many years. She's become somewhat of an expert at dabbling with personal horoscopes.

Star gazing Babs however – the Queen of the Crystal Ball – could transform her business with a monthly personal horoscope podcast, a StarCast. She could deliver a 10- to 15-minute personal forecast to clients wherever they are in the world.

Be a pioneer

If, like Barbara "Crystal" Ball, you're an expert in the astrology field, this is fantastic, new and uncharted territory. Because podcasting is in its infancy, you'd be a pioneer – a trendsetter, just like our puppy training podcaster earlier on.

If you are one of my budding freelance podcast entrepreneurs, I'm sure it wouldn't take you long to find an astrologer who would fit the bill for your new StarCast business.

It's written in the stars

StarCast is a unique service because it gives the listener a very personal service. It's their own radio show – all about them and what's potentially about to happen to them! How's that for Radio on Demand? Furthermore, a highly personalised service like the StarCast would almost certainly attract clients who would be prepared to pay a small subscription for a glimpse into their future on their personal radio programme.

Before too long Barbara "Crystal" Ball could have thousands of clients – a fan base large enough to expand her horizons into books, newspapers and television. Through podcasting, she's suddenly emerging as a new star! And she could also get her podcast sponsored by linking up with those supplying the world of the mysterious. She could create more opportunities. Her own brand of Crystal Ball, for instance, could be sold (through the podcast) to her subscribers ... "Barbara's Crystal Balls!"

Remember

Yes. Celebrities can turn podcasts into gold (the Rumplestiltskin effect) ... but also, golden podcasters can turn themselves into celebrities. It works both ways. And never forget the golden rules of broadcasting – inform, but above all, entertain. Be bold, be brash, be witty – develop your own personality – never sound half-hearted or dull. You've got me – don't lose me!

The future's yours

With our StarCast concept, you won't simply be looking into the future ... you'll be the future.

The TheatreCast…

Almost every major town and city has a theatre or entertainment venue. Theatres, concert arenas, and exhibition halls are potentially a vast, yet totally untapped source, of podcasting business. Take theatres, for instance. No matter how large or small, each one will have its own established website – the perfect launching pad for your new radio show, or TheatreCast.

The Empire strikes back!

Let's invent an imaginary theatre – The Empire in the heart of Podcastershire. Here, the press office will produce a brochure for the theatre's forthcoming attractions. They will often send out press releases to local radio and television stations as well as advertise in the local newspapers.

As my budding podcasting entrepreneur, your job is relatively simple. You're going to turn that What's On brochure into a quality radio show and deliver it direct to the Empire's customers … as well as other theatregoers around the world.

You're giving the Empire Theatre its very own radio station.

Creating your TheatreCast

The broadcast will consist of the venue's future star attractions. A Wireless What's On. As always, sex the show up a bit. Take small sound bites from the theatre manager explaining how fantastic his venue's next production will be – how many costumes they're going to use and how expensive and lavish the sets will be.

As you're helping promote the productions, you may well get permission to use music from the shows to enhance the broadcast. What a great way to beat the musical minefield we spoke of earlier. There might even be a chance for you to go out to the theatre to interview the stars (remember we've already mentioned the benefit of an 'outside broadcast').

Entertain and inform

The box office number will, of course, be featured prominently – as will the Empire Theatre's website page. But don't be afraid to delve a little deeper. Investigate the personalities 'behind the scenes' at the theatre – make stars of the staff and help them develop their own identities. Bring the theatre to life on its own radio station.

Passionate theatregoers will soon be having such a good time hearing about their favourite subject – they won't realise that they are, in effect, listening to a What's On advert from the Empire.

ENCORE! Everybody wins!

It's a two-way thing

As with all podcasts, remember never to separate the broadcast from the listener. In the TheatreCast there can be a section where punters leave reviews of past shows they have watched and enjoyed.

How Much?

The TheatreCast need not cost the theatre or entertainment venue a penny. In fact, as well as providing their local culture vultures with a brand new service – they could be making a bit on the side.

Like every podcaster it's their radio station – they can have advertisements on it if they so wish. "Next time you visit Podcastershire, make sure you stay in the Carlton Hotel – within easy reach of the theatre" or "Why not take the bus to the theatre? – Podcast Coaches will deliver you to the door."

The CommuniCast…

Even small, village notice board style broadcasts have a valuable place in the podcast community, and they too can be sponsored on a smaller scale.

Community or church parish podcasting, in time, will take the place of the village newsletter. Local shops and services were always happy to advertise in the parish magazines of old – how electrifying for them to take their place on a world stage.

What a thrill for our local butcher, Mr Podman, who will be able to hear his first ever radio announcement.

Mr Podman's bangers will be simply bursting with excitement, and for the listeners – it will be like being part of a new, extended family. Podcasting can bring the community back together like never before.

Remember

Once you're up and running either producing or presenting a podcast for one group of people, don't be afraid to expand. As your reputation begins to grow and word of mouth starts to spread, steadily build up your client base and your podcast empire could begin to sprout up before your very eyes.

And don't forget to combine the ideas in this book. Use the PodFlash to expand your service – so at the touch of a button, your listeners can be kept up to date with any breaking news … in a flash.

The NewsCast …

Many newspapers, worldwide, are quickly latching on to the podcast explosion. They see it as a fascinating way to capture new readers and help spread the headlines of the day.

So where do I fit in?

Imagine how the free weekly newspapers could benefit from a regular podcast. Now, suddenly, all of their readers can become listeners too. They can have their news 'on the go' wherever they are in the world. The broadcast could simply be posted onto a local newspaper's website for readers to download free of charge. Or, if they wish, the reader can have the radio show delivered every week, again free, through one of the world's aggregators or podcatchers.

The Podcaster Gazette!

The Podcaster Gazette, for instance, is a free weekly newspaper for the borough of Podcastershire. Your podcast can complement the newspaper – giving listeners an idea of what's to come in this week's edition. It will help promote the paper and can carry news, views, and competitions. The Podcaster Gazette could encourage readers to become listeners by means of a new ingenious form of competition – one question in the newspaper and one in the podcast, but you have to answer both questions to win the prize.

Making stars of everybody

Encourage the correspondents of the newspaper to get involved in your podcast. Make stars of them. After all, they wrote the stories. Your journalists on the Podcaster Gazette will love taking part. Many of them will be hankering after a job in radio as part of the next stage in their careers. Now they've got the chance to hone their skills.

Bringing people together

Imagine the delight of former Podcastershire people who have moved away from the area. They can now keep bang up-to-date with the goings-on in their home town, wherever they are in the world ... and it won't cost them a penny. The podcast could even become a regular feature in the paper. Who's listening? Where are they? What job did they used to have in the town? Why did they move away?

News or sport

Sports news could also feature highly. If you're going for the evening newspaper market, why not concentrate on the sports section of the publication?

A weekly podcast, backed by the paper, could keep local sports fans up-to-date with the goings-on at their club (similar to our earlier SportsCast but this time covering many clubs or sports in one area). Wherever they are geographically, listeners could have their programme delivered to them to listen whenever and wherever they wished. It will be just like going back home again once a week.

Remember

Every time you broadcast put on a performance. Make sure everyone who appears behind the microphone sounds bright and bubbly. Keep them in the performance zone at all times. Yours might be the most important message in the whole world, and unless it's delivered with passion and authority, it won't be heard.

A NewsCast goldmine – part one

All newspapers carry adverts – it's how they make their living. Now that The Podcaster Gazette has burst into life as a radio show, no end of small and not so small businesses will queue up to send their message to the world ... on Radio Podcaster Gazette!

Even the classified advertisements like the births, marriages and deaths could have their own spot. How's that? You can now announce your marriage in the newspaper and have the news broadcast around the world by podcast. It's the perfect match!

Potential advertisers will now get the chance to deliver their message, through your NewsCast, direct to their customers. Readers might miss a newspaper advertisement – listeners can't possibly miss a podcast advert. It's right there ... it hits them right between the ears.

A NewsCast goldmine – part two

Already we've investigated the notion of sports stars and pop stars talking direct to their fans via podcast. National newspapers could easily make use of this type of podcast to massive effect.

They could make celebrity messages instantly available to all of their readers, downloaded directly from the newspaper website straight onto to the readers' iPods or MP3 players.

If the paper has signed up a star as a world exclusive – it can broadcast the star's message as well as print it. The same could go for the release of a new song ... a free podcast (a gift from the paper to its readers) with the pop star introducing his or her new hit, direct and exclusively to fans worldwide – via the newspaper's free podcast service. "Listen all about it!", "Listen all about it!"

The PodComic …

Don't forget the massive kids' market. Remember the excitement and anticipation when your favourite comic used to arrive at the newsagent. Multiply that feeling more than 1,000 times and you've still not got a flavour of this thrilling new product, which could shake the valuable youth market to its very core.

Eureka! We've created a completely new invention – the PodComic! But wait – it's even better than that. Everyone can read a comic or watch the television. With an iPod or an MP3 player, our youngsters of today can now listen to a message from their heroes... one to one.

This time – it's personal!

Kids can subscribe free of charge to have a 10-minute broadcast, tailored to their own specific interest – pop gossip, soccer training, the latest card collecting craze, anything. Whenever a new show comes out, it will be downloaded direct to them – all they have to do is listen to their favourite stars talking directly to them about their favourite subjects..

It's happening!

Podcasting is not just for the 'teeny-podders'. In October 2004, a Google search would have returned fewer than 6,000 results for podcasting.

By August 2005 that number had risen to over ten million. In May 2007, if you enter podcasting into your Google directory, you'll come up with 33.5 million entries.

chapter 11
My cheeky top ten

Have a giggle at these hooks. I've included them to demonstrate that there are potential podcasting ideas everywhere. Indeed, just a two-minute glance through the current crop of radio shows gracing the podcast-o-sphere, threw up the following unique, wacky, and sometimes mind blowing menu.

They include gems like: The Traditional Art of Hedge Laying, Camping and Caravanning (including the 'tip of the week' and the 'weekly cocktail'), Mr Thrifty's Frugal Living, 101 Ways with a Turnip, Gossip Over the Garden Gate, Breastfeeding ... and Why God is Scottish! There's even a show called Naughty Sheets where the presenters broadcast in the nude!

Here are some others ...

1. The PodQuiz

Earlier on in this book we mentioned that podcasting has no rules. "You can just sneeze into the microphone once a week if you like", I said. But wait a moment. If that sneeze was a celebrity sneeze, then you've got the makings of a brand new type of podcast – a world first. The PodQuiz.

"Who's the sneezer, geezer?" It's a show where members of the public could win big prizes for guessing the identity of your mystery celebrity sneezers. You can have lots of fun with the PodQuiz. Mystery voices, sounds or even the Secret Santa at Christmas – get creative! The PodQuiz is on its way ... any questions?

2. The GodCast

The newspapers will love this. The world's first batch of GodCasters.

Hallelujah

It does exactly what it says on the tin. A religious message, delivered direct to your MP3 player / iPod or computer. Religious leaders of all denominations are always quick to warn us of falling attendances at their places of worship. GodCasts reverse that trend by taking the church, or any other place of worship, directly to the people.

A member of the clergy can simply record a sermon or religious message and send it direct to his or her flock. After all "If the mountain will not come to Mohammed, Mohammed will go to the mountain."

Stars on Sunday

The brightest media friendly ministers will do extremely well from a weekly GodCast. An all singing / all dancing broadcast that still manages to get the message across effectively – but in a new, absorbing fashion.

The GodCast can be as adventurous as you like. Small-scale community church podcasts can be just that!

But the more successful GodCasters will undoubtedly go on to create shows where people will pay to listen. They may well become stars in their own right, spreading the message all over the world (it's what podcasting was made for!).

3. The LoveCast

Hello, hello, hello! This one is just for the adults. Perk up your sex life on podcast. Don't forget, the show is delivered direct to your computer ... so there's no need for plain brown envelopes! You could even be listening to the tips while you're at it! (But don't let the headphones get in the way.)

Of course, relationships are not all about sex. What about dating tips? How to successfully romance the man or woman of your dreams. There's even room for a series of podcasts leading up to your wedding day to make sure everything goes smoothly. (Featuring any number of adverts from photographers, car hire specialists ... and chimney sweeps!)

And finally, after the honeymoon, your baby and toddler podcast tips – a weekly podcast that grows with your child!

4. The PubCast

It's a great way to create a unique sound for your podcast and make money by getting creative with your listeners. Base your shows in a good old-fashioned boozer (that's a public house in England or a café bar on the continent). You can either create an imaginary pub in your studio or go out and set up in a real one, with the permission of a friendly landlord. Talk to – and about – your pub regulars and build up their parts in the podcast.

When word spreads, why not suggest to your listeners that, instead of paying to download your shows, they should dip into their pockets and buy you a drink. The presenters could mention the names of listeners that have 'donated' money for a pint, by raising a glass to them.

If you want to take it one stage further, why not ask for sponsorship from the brewers of your favourite tipple. Cheers ... !

5. The FatCast

Keeping in trim has become a way of life for many of us. Hundreds of booming businesses have been created by the keep fit phenomenon and the dieting business. There's a fortune to be made in flab fighting.

Now, hold on to your scales, because here comes a radical, new weekly dieting regime – courtesy of the podcast.

It's the FatCast!! ... and it's absolutely mouth watering.

Direct dieting

No more daunting treks to the local dieting club. Your whole weekly or monthly diet programme can now be delivered straight onto your computer and downloaded directly onto your portable device.

We're all different – there are many thousands of diets to accompany many millions of individual tastes and lifestyles. There can be just as many FatCasts. The better ones will grow into cult broadcasts – the new 'must have' dieting accessory for the weight conscious.

Similarly, the best dieting broadcasters, the most inspirational and motivational speakers, will turn into cult stars. Who knows what their groundbreaking podcasts will turn into – books, television shows? You name it.

Remember

You can use podcasting as your launch pad to fame and fortune. There can be no better place to develop and fine-tune your considerable broadcasting skills.

Imagine that ...

The FatCast will enable weight conscious men, women and even children to follow their own specific diet in the comfort of their own homes – and monitor their progress as the system updates month by month, or even week by week.

Already thousands of magazines are making a fortune through flab fighting, now the podcast revolution is set to take off where magazines fear to tread.

Becoming a fat cat!

FatCasts could easily be sponsored by one of the many global companies that supply dieting products or have their own flab fighting publications. Maybe a diet or health magazine would be prepared to launch its own podcast service – thus promoting itself around the world and helping its readers shed their pounds at the same time.

6. The MumCast

Sounds simple doesn't it? A show made by mothers focussing entirely on motherhood. But, amazingly, this type of podcast is proving to be one of the most successful and lucrative in the whole of the United States.

Two mothers in Virginia, with seven children between them but no broadcasting experience, set up a MumCast a few months ago (check it out ... **www.mommycast.com**). The programme became instantly successful and now they have two major commercial sponsors.

Never mind 'don't give up your day job', if two ordinary mums from America can do it – surely anyone can, no matter where they live or what they're podcasting about!

7. The FitCast

Keep Fit or Yoga classes by podcast! Watch out, they're on their way. A complete workout in the comfort of your own home, with musical accompaniment and your own, personal instructor.

Even celebrities could climb aboard the bandwagon as guest instructors – popping directly into your lives every week to help you keep in trim on a one-to-one level.

And remember, you don't have to leave the comfort of your front room for your next keep-fit session. Once you've subscribed to the show, every new FitCast drops straight onto your computer. What a great platform for health food companies or the keep fit industry to advertise their products and services. A direct hit to the people who are most likely to buy their goods.

8. The CookCast

We've already discussed the notion of cookery in podcast form. The CookCast, however, could transform the old, established world of the battered and beaten cookery books. It's time to take recipes off the page and into the podcast.

CookCasts could bring any recipe bursting into life. You'll almost be able to smell the apple turnover! Remember, the beauty of podcasting is that the shows are Radio on Demand; budding chefs could listen to their favourite programmes wherever they are, whenever they want to, even in the kitchen. CookCasts could represent the biggest shake up in the cooking industry since the invention of the tossed salad. And it will happen. The bigger the celebrity chef, the bigger the audience and the larger the sponsorship.

"Podcasting is leading the Radio on Demand revolution. It gives listeners exactly what they want to hear – when they want to hear it."

9. The BuffCast

Within a relatively short space of time, there will be a podcast for every single group or hobby.

Imagine you're in a newsagent. Spend a minute taking a look at the magazine titles. There are literally hundreds, possibly hundreds of thousands worldwide, reflecting the millions of hobbies that tickle the fancy of a human race with a zillion different interests. We're all different; we all have our own passions and fancies.

Very soon, every single one of those magazines will become a specialist podcast – it's starting to happen already. Where magazines once led the way, podcasting will soon take over. Every subject you can possibly imagine will soon be explored by an expert on podcast ... even a broadcast exclusively for those who like to shed their clothing.

Naturists rejoice ... the BuffCast is on its way!

Remember

The most bizarre, unique, or entertaining programmes will become the most successful podcasts. The more you stand out, the more publicity you'll get – and the more people will want to listen. These podcasts will attract the biggest audiences and the most high profile sponsors ... they'll probably also make the most money for their presenters and producers.

10. The CharityCast

Earlier on in this chapter, we discussed the possibility of making money through 'donations' from your new family of listeners (remember the PubCast and the buy us a drink idea).

More and more podcasters are deciding to go down the donations route rather than ask for a fixed fee from their listeners to download a show. A pair of film buffs, for example, have created their CineCast podcast empire. If you go to their website: **www.cinecast.com** you will se that there is a PayPal button for donations from listeners who enjoy their shows. PayPal has a superb reputation and offers a great way for accepting such donations.

Charities could also use this method for getting the messages and appeals across and collecting donations at the same time.

The unstoppable march of the Podcast

The more established and popular hobbies – take angling for example – will have dozens of different radio shows. Fishermen and women worldwide will soon get their own specific radio broadcast delivered direct to their computers. R.o.d.Casting (Radio on Demand) can easily cater for the anglers of the globe – The RodCast!

Anything and everything will soon be nestling happily beneath the podcast umbrella. From fixing your car to collecting milk bottles; from biscuit making to brain surgery; from poetry to poker; from hang gliding to hand bell ringing.

But don't wait for it to happen. Become a podcast pioneer and make it happen!

chapter 12
Making the most of yourself

So, now you know how easy it is to create a podcast. You know how to broadcast your message and how to create a hook on which to hang your new radio show.

Together, we've learnt how successful shows could make their presenters a great deal of money through paid subscription (pay-per-listen) and/or advertising. We've even introduced podcasting to the business community via the Podvert and PodFlash.

Here are a few other ways in which your newly created broadcasting talents can work for you. These working models might be just up your street...

The DramCast ...

The world of the performing arts is about to undergo the most pulsating transformation of all time. A shake-up that will take any undiscovered talent and project it onto the biggest stage – under the brightest spotlight, ever! If you're dead set on dramatics, or if you have a passion for performing – then it's time to use podcasting to make the world your stage.

Curtain up

Put yourself in the place of my imaginary theatre group – the DramCast Players. For years they've struggled to drum up audiences for their top class productions, often travelling many thousands of miles to perform their next gig in the Lower Hamble Village Hall to a handful of hardy culture vultures.

It's happening!

Here's a true story ... and a great example of how a budding author successfully used podcasting to promote his talent on a global stage.

The gentleman concerned was a frustrated writer who felt he had a bestseller on his hands but time and time again had his work turned down by publishers and film producers. He felt some of the publishers were not even reading his masterpiece before penning the dreaded rejection letter.

Undaunted, he decided to record a series of podcasts to showcase his efforts – and they became an instant hit with more than 50,000 downloads.

With this success under his belt, our unknown writer returned to his publishers.

Of course, they couldn't now refuse a man with such a large, global fan base. How could they say no to such a guaranteed hit? The book was published and, of course, the writer's new army of fans who'd heard of its publication on our hero's podcast eagerly snapped it up!

Spurred on by his achievement, the writer returned to those film producers and, sure enough, his work became a success on the silver screen.

His dreams and wishes all came true – thanks to podcasting.

Bringing it to life

All the DramCast Players need to do is set up a small podcast studio, select a play ... and perform to the world. What fun they'll have watching their work suddenly burst into life on a worldwide stage. What a thrill when they see who's been listening around the globe. What satisfaction when they see their popularity begin to soar.

The DramCast players could always encourage interaction with their new fans on their website with biographies of their leading men and women. They might even ask for feedback and audience reviews.

Your own theatre workshop

If you're a budding writer, what better place to workshop your new creation than a worldwide stage – yes, you'll probably get your critics, but all constructive feedback will prove invaluable in your quest to pen the perfect production.

Furthermore, if the DramCast Players become successful, there's every chance their new fans will pay a small fee for the next production – some shows might attract advertisers, giving them the ultimate "pay-per-listen" and sponsorship combination.

Remember

Try to keep your new work short and to the point. Although podcasting is convenient and flexible, it's likely that a one-hour production is the absolute limit for one broadcast. A 15-minute short play is excellent. Keep your new fans begging for more. "Only a fool breaks the 15 minute rule!"

The SoapCast ...

Who will be the first to create and produce the first worldwide SoapCast? It's a simple, yet exciting variation of the DramCast. Why not create and perform your own soap opera? Half a dozen, 15-minute episodes to start with – ending with the time-honoured, traditional soap-style cliffhanger.

Imagine that – the world's newest soap (or even soap 'spoof') delivered to your new soap fans around the globe instantly, at the touch of a button. Written and performed by ... you!

Creating the dream

Successful SoapCasters could achieve the podcast dream of pay-per-listen audiences and major sponsors who may well be queuing up to use your show as a platform to get their message to a worldwide audience.

As for the audience, imagine their excitement when your very latest thrilling episode drops onto their computers, MP3 players and iPods all around the globe – excitement for you and your new fans alike.

Your SoapCast fans can hear the latest episode whenever they like – in the bath, on the underground, on the train – anywhere. That's why podcasting is the perfect vehicle for a new wave of performing arts.

Spreading the word

Don't forget, when your DramCast or SoapCast has been produced, feel free to send it out to the more well established theatre, television and radio producers around the world. (That's if they haven't already picked up on it.) We're told that the entire world is a stage. Step forward and take your well-deserved bow.

The ComedyCast …

If you've got a passion for comedy, then the ComedyCast could put you on the road to stardom. At the very least it will be your first tentative step into the sometimes brutal, lonely world of the comedian.

Make them laugh

Put your act down on a podcast – or ComedyCast – after all, it's one certain way to avoid the hecklers, and bypass the crowded social clubs. You don't even have to travel miles to your next dodgy gig – instead, let the whole world come to you.

Make sure your ComedyCast is of the highest possible quality. Brush up your act and rehearse it many times over before you're happy with a polished final product.

What have you got to lose?

The beauty of podcasting is that you can have several goes before you decide on your finished programme. You don't even have to memorise your gags – have them written before you (but make yourself sound as natural as possible – not as if you're simply reading from a script). Again, why not send your finished broadcast to as many of the established television and radio producers as you possibly can. Production houses too might like to hear your quality ComedyCast.

Get to the decision makers

The ComedyCast is not just confined to the world of the stand-up comedian. It's an ideal chance for you to create all sorts of comedy shows and sketches, and deliver your work direct to the decision makers.

If you're a comedy writer – what better way to present your new ideas?

The BookCast …

Have you ever wondered why you can remember a tune you heard at breakfast time but not the article you read in the paper? That's the beauty of audio. Sound is intrusive – yet irresistible.

Therefore, if you're an author, why not send a couple of tantalising chapters of your latest work to your targeted publishers direct via podcast? They won't have to plough through realms of written work – they can listen to your book on the way home from work. Bring your manuscript to life using your new broadcasting skills. Make it stand out – hit the publishers right between the ears. It's a 'novel' idea that just might set you aside from the rest!

Always remember as a podcaster you are automatically breaking new ground. Most people will be pleasantly surprised at what you've achieved before they even listen to your work.

The ShowCast …

Showcasting is the ideal way to present yourself and your talents to the globe.

Make yourself glow

If you're applying for a job, why not create a podcast CV and promote yourself in a unique way. It's sure to set you aside from the other candidates.

Simply make a short broadcast that highlights your considerable talents and qualifications. Let your personality shine through – use it to win the vacant position. You can simply send your broadcast direct to the decision makers via email attachment.

Make your CV show short, informative and entertaining – make sure you sound like the sort of employee that no company could do without.

Congratulations! You're hired …

Although this book firmly believes in podcasting challenging conventional radio in the next few years, you still might like to chase a career on the old-fashioned wireless.

Go on then, do it! Send a sample of your radio talents to the stations of your choice but make sure your ShowCast is no longer than ten minutes – and be sure you know which stations to pick. It's no good sending an all-speech show to a music station.

"All over the world, radio listeners are slinging the schedules. People power is embracing the podcast revolution.

The Ex-Factor

Podcasting will create hundreds of new rock and pop stars – fact!

Why not bypass the old fashioned, outdated X-Factor type talent shows. There's no need for you to queue up alongside thousands of hopefuls waiting for your minute in front of the spotlight. That's just a lottery. This sort of talent show is old hat – don't be part of the cattle market, use a regular podcast to jump the queue.

Be smart. Put your music down on a ShowCast and deliver it straight to the music industry's top movers and shakers.

Top of the pods!

As mentioned earlier, blog sites – like **www.myspace.com** or **www.youtube.com** - are superb for new bands wanting to showcase their talent.

You don't need to break the bank and you don't need much computer know-how. Just join the blog site, perform ... and watch the blog community spread the word. What a fantastic way to get your music heard and create a fan base across the world.

I firmly believe that, even in this hectic day and age, true talent will always shine through. Record companies and agents will soon come knocking on the doors of the most successful artists.

To take it a stage further, if you're a singer or a member of a rock or pop band, you can enhance your global fan base by creating your own full scale podcast show – talk about your music, introduce your band members and let their personalities shine through.

Introduce yourself to the world

Podcasting is the perfect way to present yourself to the world. And it won't cost the earth! Congratulations. You've arrived.

chapter 13
The world is waiting…

I've given you an awful lot to take on board in this publication. It's almost the end of your podcast journey … and the beginning of your podcast adventure so, for now, we can afford to let our hair down. Let me prove, once and for all, there are no podcasting limits. Let's have some fun investigating the ultimate podcasts … You're about to realise that podcasting is most definitely 'Reality radio on speed'!

The CelebCast

Podcasting will revolutionise the world's biggest business — that of the celebrity. Forget the glossy magazines, they're about to become old news. What about a new world where you can really get inside the lives of your favourite superstars? Even better, have them talk direct to you every week or month. It's a dream come true for the fans who, at long last, will be given an exclusive glimpse into the world of the Hollywood superstar, the rock kings and queens —or even the latest super-couple.

It's a glossy celebrity magazine brought to life by the Celebs themselves. Once again we've turned the media world on its head. CelebCasts will become a worldwide phenomenon. It's a dream for the fans and a broadcasting goldmine for the podcast pioneers. Forget the television, conventional radio and newspapers. As predicted, we've burst through the barriers.

I wonder who'll be the first stars to begin talking direct to their fans … ear-to-ear, one-to-one! And I wonder who'll line up in the first batch of podcast millionaires.

The PoshCast

Here's an example of an ultimate CelebCast.

Take one super couple (a famous footballer and a former pop singing megastar, for example). Now, turn that celebrity couple into our ultimate podcasters with a weekly or monthly 15-minute broadcast outlining the various shenanigans and goings-on in their star-studded ultra-glamorous lives.

Go shopping with the lady of the house and play football with king of the spin (or should that be bend?). What makes the pair of them tick? Where have they been? Who have they been with?

A PoshCast would create massive publicity for the couple involved, along with worldwide listeners – and huge sponsorship into the bargain.

The RoyalCast

To push the boundaries still further – how about this one...

The goings-on in Britain's Royal household – brought to you directly, every month. A ridiculous notion, you might think. But wait a moment. There are no rules for the ongoing march of the podcast pioneer. Podcasting is introducing the world to a massive range of new ideas and opportunities.

What better way for the Royal family to talk to their subjects directly ... and not through press speculation. Even the Queen's Christmas broadcast is now made into a podcast – freely available around the world to listen to, not just on Christmas day itself, but whenever you fancy it.

Her Majesty could quickly become one of my budding pioneers. The QueenCast is on its way!

PodLegends

Remember when we were discussing the SportsCast we mentioned a series called the PodLegends? Who will be the first to record a series of podcasts about the life and times of various sporting, music, television, or film stars? A film or pop star's life, brought to life on a podcast would be irresistible to fans the world over. Don't buy the biography – download it and listen at your leisure. It's Desert Island Discs brought into the new era. The PodLegends series could become cult listening – and turn the show's presenter into the new Michael Parkinson!

Animal crackers

Who's going to be the first animal broadcasting legend? A sheep, a horse, a frog, a cockerel, or a pod cat? The idea is not as daft as you might think. Johnny Morris used to bring animals to life in his television show Animal Magic. Likewise safari parks, zoos and nature centres, could create their own animal radio shows, and the world's first collection of animal mega-stars. Imagine if a zoo created a monthly podcast featuring its animals as the stars.

The venue would receive massive publicity, both from the podcast itself and from newspapers reporting on its existence. It could also achieve cult status among listeners, and therefore, help pull in more people through the gates.

Remember

Podcasting has no tried and tested formula. Furthermore, whatever the subject, it immediately catapults the have-a-go broadcaster onto a level playing field with the broadcasting legends.

The AlienCast

Possibly the ultimate podcast … unless, of course, you know different!

One enterprising American astronaut has already made the world's first SpaceCast. Who is going to be the world's first alien radio star? Again, it's a publicity goldmine – the whole world will want to have a piece of the action. Who could resist listening to a 'real-life' alien, broadcasting from his or her own planet (wherever that might be?). It's not impossible. You might already be an alien. If so, brand yourself and get broadcasting from your own planet!

Promotion, promotion, promotion

Whatever subject you decide to broadcast on, the vital element in generating the largest possible audience (and potentially maximum revenue) is getting your podcast noticed. It doesn't matter how exceptional your radio show is or how much of a dazzling broadcaster you are – if nobody knows your show exists, you won't get any listeners. Guaranteed!

Get yourself promoted as much as possible. Spread the word using as many devices as you can. Get your show listed in iTunes and with as many other podcast directories, podcatchers or aggregators (whatever you chose to call them) as possible.

You need to let people know you are out there to achieve a large audience.

And when you've achieved a large audience, you can then start to think about ways to make the maximum amount of money from your new skills through pay-per-listen, sponsorship, advertising on your website, or donation.

chapter 14
Bon voyage!

You are about to launch yourself into a new and exciting world. You could be about to transform your life for good. Whether you use your new skills as a fulfilling hobby or a new career, we wish you all the luck in the world ... and don't forget, the world is now your podcasting playground.

Above all ... have fun!

Go for gold... podcasting gold

You might be about to use your new talents to transform yourself into a major broadcasting star. You might be launching your pop band or drama group onto a world stage.

Whatever the case, Podcasting is set to create hundreds of new stars. It's a fact.

Alternatively, you might want to use our hints and tips to set up your own stable of podcast shows and presenters.

You might be thinking of using the Podvert or PodFlash to set up a new company helping businesses to promote their goods and services on a global stage.

If you're about to embark on any kind of podcasting career, here are some final thoughts to send you on your way ...

The podcast top twenty

1 Podcasting puts you at the forefront of a radio revolution.

2 It gives you the chance to talk to the world – and prove your talents on a global stage. Where better to launch your new broadcasting career?

3 Radio on Demand. It's the buzz phrase for a new generation of broadcasting giants. The podcast satisfies the listeners' need for Radio on Demand. The phrase 'tune in' will soon be condemned to the broadcasters' recycle bin.

4 Nearly all radio stars of the future will be hand-plucked from the growing band of podcast pioneers.

5 Don't miss out on your chance to achieve your wildest dream. If you've got something to say ... say it to the world!

6 Remember our golden rules of broadcasting. Inform, but above all, entertain. Keep in the performance zone throughout your show.

7 Be bold, brash and witty – develop your own personality and connect with your audience ... they are your extended family so care for them. Be funny, be angry, be peculiar and be intriguing. Try to stand out from the crowd. But don't try to be cool.

8 Always leave room for a sequel. Leave the listener desperate to embark on their next exciting adventure with you.

9 Because it's so new, becoming a podcaster immediately catapults you onto a level playing field with the big boys of the broadcasting industry. Congratulations. You are now standing shoulder to shoulder with your radio heroes.

10 The most talented, unique or entertaining shows will quickly gather an army of admirers who might be prepared to pay to listen to your words of wisdom.

11 Cult podcasts will attract huge audiences worldwide. Huge audiences will attract massive pay-per-listen subscription ... and sponsorship in the form of lucrative adverts. Paid for subscription (pay-per-listen) and programme sponsorship (adverts) are the dream combination for a podcast pioneer.

12 Because podcasting gives you an instant global audience – it's irresistible for business leaders. The Podvert and PodFlash are set to revolutionise the world of advertising, bringing a company's product or service to life on a worldwide stage.

13 Podcast entrepreneurs will become the thrusting new generation of broadcasting giants. They'll follow in the footsteps of the dot-com pioneers who trod exciting new paths before them.

14 Businesses are only just waking up to the podcast explosion. Presenting your idea will be exciting for them. Tell them how they'll be at the forefront of a new broadcasting era. Explain what an exciting, new and relatively untapped medium they now have for spreading the word.

15 A celebrity-based podcast will boost your audience significantly. CelebCasts could soon become a worldwide phenomenon.

16 Original ideas will create podcast millionaires.

17 The rampant march of the podcast knows no limits and has no boundaries.

18 Podcasting has no rules – every day the wheel is being re-invented by the world's first batch of podcast pioneers. Change the rules whenever you like – create your own!

19 YOU are the next greatest thing – and you're about to be discovered. Don't just sit there – create a podcast and show the world how great you are!

20 Always remember ... the world is waiting. What are you waiting for?

PS … The future!

I want to leave you with an outline of my personal vision for the future of podcasting … so here we go!

Fad or fab?

Congratulations on your impeccable timing. You've joined the radio revolution at its pivotal point. Podcasting is on the brink – it's at the crossroads … so just what is going to happen next?

The good, the bad …

The good news is that there are more than enough listeners to cope with the impending podcast explosion. The bad news is that the term 'podcasting' is confusing. Furthermore, it doesn't do the phenomenon any favours at all. It's nowhere near dynamic, exciting or romantic enough. Podcasting needs to be rebranded … any ideas?

… and the ugly!

The listeners may be there – but there simply aren't enough GOOD QUALITY shows for them to download. Furthermore, there are so many podcasts that the best shows are getting drowned in a sea of radio dross.

Listeners who visit podcast hosting sites are so overwhelmed by the sheer volume of poor shows to pick from that they often give up the hunt before they find a golden nugget. The most talented broadcasters need to be plucked out and given the spotlight.

Radio Heaven

MENU

Home

From our Archives

Any Questions?

Channel Guide

Celebrity Channel

Lifestyle Channel

Aliens Only Channel

Contact Us

Click Here To
JOIN NOW!

Members login here:
sername:
assword:

Login

Welcome to Radio Heaven

Congratulations ! You've tuned in to RadioHeaven.com, the world's first celebrity podcast radio station, producing quality shows for your iPods and MP3 players.

RadioHeaven.com features the biggest stories and star secrets direct and exclusive, from some of the world's most famous celebrity names.

Quite simply, RadioHeaven.com takes you straight to the superstars at the click of a button.

It's your glossy celebrity magazine on the radio - for you to download and listen whenever ... and wherever you like!

RadioHeaven.com is a pioneering world first ... the only radio station in the universe which allows you to tap directly into the minds and thoughts of your favourite celebrities.

From music making legends to the idols of the silver screen - all the big names are here waiting to tell you their own fascinating stories.

**- Have a listen and tell your friends -
Visit RadioHeaven.com...
Home of the Stars!**

Click here for an audio welcome to RadioHeaven.com

Your featured Celebrities:

DONNY OSMOND
...And they call it Puppy Love! Click here to find out how teen idol Donny Osmond conquered the awful demons that threatened his career. What it was like growing up in the world's most famous family? And what happened during a secret meeting with Michael Jackson.

GENE PITNEY
...And he was only, 24 hours from Tulsa! Click here to find out how pop legend Gene Pitney made his millions through music - and it was all thanks to a bizarre twist of fate ... And can you spot the deliberate mistake in his worldwide best seller?

JOAN SIMS
...Oh, what a Carry On! Legend of the silver screen and Great Britain's national treasure Joan Sims reveals the secrets behind the Carry On phenomenon... and why she turned down an astonishing proposal from Kenneth Williams.

MORE, MORE, MORE...
Click here for a galaxy of other stars featured today on RadioHeaven.com, including:

"The story of Mowtown" by Martha Reeves
"The Phantom of the floorboards!" by Michael Crawford
"From Leicester to Las Vegas" by Engelburt Humperdinck.

Introducing RadioHeaven.com

RadioHeaven.com is unique and is set to take the podcasting revolution from mayhem ... to mainstream. It is the first 'radio station on the Internet' and is dedicated to the cream of the podcast crop. Home to the world's first celebrity podcasts, **RadioHeaven.com** features shows and exclusive snippets from some of the most famous pop legends, comedy stars and sporting heroes. Listeners have only the best to select from.

RadioHeaven.com is the future. No longer will you have to trawl through thousands of poor shows before reaching a gem.

Changing your life

RadioHeaven.com is also the only radio station in the world that can improve your life for good! It contains a series of life-changing broadcasts, providing tips on everything ... from how to look after your garden, to how to become a successful human being! If you need help with your pets or even a boost in the bedroom, the hand picked, expert presenters on RadioHeaven.com are there to help you negotiate all of life's little (and not so little) dilemmas.

The future is bright

Of course, the odd-ball ranters and the niche market amateurs will continue to thrive in the podcast revolution. But these new ultra professional podcast stables like RadioHeaven.com will lead the transformation from fad to fab! Podcasting (or whatever we choose to call it) will soon be competing shoulder to shoulder with conventional radio for new listeners worldwide ... and winning hands down! Long live the revolution!

Your podcasting alphabet …

A **Audacity**. A computer programme that records and edits your radio show. It's easy to download and it's the choice of many top professionals. Furthermore, it won't cost you a penny.

B **Blogging**. It's how podcasting first began. Blog sites are a special kind of website containing a person's journal or online personal diary. When the bloggers got bored with writing down their thoughts, they developed a way of broadcasting them to the world – audio-blogging (or podcasting) was born!

C **Chicklet**. A slang term for those little orange buttons that have the letters XML or RSS in them. Used by podcatchers or aggregators on their directories to allow listeners to easily subscribe to a radio show of their choice … at the click of a chicklet!

D **Delivery boys**. What makes your podcast special is the way in which it's delivered to listeners around the world. Aggregators or Podcatchers are the fairy godmothers of the podcasting world. They sprinkle the woofle dust onto your podcast. They deliver your show and any further episodes direct to your listener free of charge, using RSS feeds.

E **Email**. Podcasts have never previously been distributed by email – until now. We've rewritten the rule book. The PodFlash is a two minute podcast that can easily be sent out to your email clients on attachment.

F **FTP**. File Transfer Program. You'll need one of these to upload your radio shows and broadcasts onto the internet. Don't despair; there are many FTP programs available on the Internet – and sites to help you.

G **Geek Speak**. Forget it! Podcasting is for broadcasters … not techno-bores!

H **Hooks**. Content is crucial. Always find a hook to hang your broadcast on. Ask yourself "What am I passionate about?" The answer to that question could be the subject of your podcast.

I **iPod**. A digital media player from Apple Computers. The name inspired the term podcasting. MP3 players do virtually the same job.

J **Juice**. **http://juicereceiver.sourceforge.net**. This was one of the original podcast aggregators set up to download new shows to listeners worldwide whenever they became available. Juice still boasts to be "the premier podcast receiver."

K **Kit!** To set up your radio station you'll need a computer, microphone, adequate soundcard, a handful of computer programs, which can be easily downloaded (often free of charge), and a set of headphones (optional). USB microphones are becoming increasingly popular among podcasters. They plug directly into the USB port at the back of the computer (USB stands for Universal Serial Bus).

L **LAME MP3 Encoder**. A free and simple to download computer programme that converts your recordings and radio shows into MP3 formats, ready for them to be uploaded onto the internet – and downloaded by your army of new fans.

M **MP3**. Originally known as an "MPEG_1 Audio Layer 3". It's the technology that compresses a sound sequence into a very small audio file while preserving the quality of that file to almost that of a conventional CD.

Niche markets. Podcasting is ideal for reaching specific areas of interest. If you create your own niche market, your broadcast will soon become a powerful source of information and enjoyment for your listeners.

Originality. Remember, the more original and entertaining the radio show – the more it will stand out from the crowd, giving you more chance of success.

Podcasting. Creating a radio show on the Internet that can be delivered to listeners across the world with the help of podcatchers or aggregators. A podcast is simply an audio file (radio show) that can be listened to on an iPod, Mp3 player, or computer.

Quick-fix podcasting. Many blog sites make podcasting easy. They'll provide broadcasters with a webpage and handle the technology to upload your radio shows onto the Internet and distribute them. These 'Quick Fix' podcasts are brilliant for the first timer or hobbyist.

RSS. Really Simple Syndication. When you've signed up with an aggregator (or podcatcher), they will ask you for a description of your radio show – an RSS feed. Then they'll start distributing your broadcast, free of charge, to anyone who subscribes to it. R was originally going to stand for rules – but in podcasting – there are no rules!

Skype. Originally an Internet telephone service that now offers a free download, enabling people to create a "Skypecast". It's another form of podcast. The friendly folk at www.skype.com offer: "A new way to have conversations with people across the world who share your interests – and it's free!"

Tag (ID3). Geeks would tell you this is a 'metadata specification'. It's simply a label for your broadcast once you've converted it into an MP3 format. When you've turned your radio show into an MP3 file, the ID3 Tag will ask you to label it. Often the name of the broadcaster, title of the show and your website address are all that's needed.

URL. Your full website address. For example **http://www.radioheaven.com**. URL stands for Uniform Resource Locator.

Volume. Always keep your volume constant. Clipping and popping are the arch enemies of the professional broadcaster. Make sure you dispose of these two villains in every broadcast!

Website. You'll need a website to air (or 'publish' if you prefer the term) your radio show. Blog sites will give you a webpage often free of charge. Otherwise you can pick your own website with its unique domain address – giving your station its own original brand.

XML. The language of the RSS feed that's understood by both humans and computers. It won't really affect you in the slightest, but at least it's useful for the podcast alphabet – it's always difficult to find an X!

Youtube.com. Where you'll find the new VodCasters. Now you've conquered the podcast, get set for a new revolution – the Vodcast (video on demand). Already, websites like Youtube.com are providing a platform for a new breed of television presenter.

ZenCasting. Podcasting by another name. It's just a term coined by Podcasters and Vodcasters using the Zen media device from Creative.

Index

'The Greatest Tips in the World' books

Baby & Toddler Tips
by Vicky Burford
ISBN 978-1-905151-70-7

Barbeque Tips
by Raymond van Rijk
ISBN 978-1-905151-68-4

Cat Tips by Joe Inglis
ISBN 978-1-905151-66-0

Cookery Tips
by Peter Osborne
ISBN 978-1-905151-64-6

Cricketing Tips
by R. Rotherham & G. Clifford
ISBN 978-1-905151-18-9

DIY Tips
by Chris Jones & Brian Lee
ISBN 978-1-905151-62-2

Dog Tips by Joe Inglis
ISBN 978-1-905151-67-7

Etiquette & Dining Tips
by Prof. R. Rotherham
ISBN 978-1-905151-21-9

Freelance Writing Tips
by Linda Jones
ISBN 978-1-905151-17-2

Gardening Tips
by Steve Brookes
ISBN 978-1-905151-60-8

Genealogy Tips
by M. Vincent-Northam
ISBN 978-1-905151-72-1

Golfing Tips
by John Cook
ISBN 978-1-905151-63-9

Horse & Pony Tips
by Joanne Bednall
ISBN 978-1-905151-19-6

Household Tips
by Vicky Burford
ISBN 978-1-905151-61-5

Personal Success Tips
by Brian Larcher
ISBN 978-1-905151-71-4

Podcasting Tips
by Malcolm Boyden
ISBN 978-1-905151-75-2

Property Developing Tips
by F. Morgan & P Morgan
ISBN 978-1-905151-69-1

Retirement Tips
by Tony Rossiter
ISBN 978-1-905151-28-8

Sex Tips
by Julie Peasgood
ISBN 978-1-905151-74-5

Travel Tips
by Simon Worsfold
ISBN 978-1-905151-73-8

Yoga Tips
by D. Gellineau & D. Robson
ISBN 978-1-905151-65-3

Pet Recipe books

The Greatest Feline Feasts in the World by Joe Inglis
ISBN 978-1-905151-50-9

The Greatest Doggie Dinners in the World by Joe Inglis
ISBN 978-1-905151-51-6

'The Greatest in the World' DVDs

The Greatest in the World – Gardening Tips
presented by Steve Brookes

The Greatest in the World – Yoga Tips
presented by David Gellineau and David Robson

The Greatest in the World – Cat & Kitten Tips
presented by Joe Inglis

The Greatest in the World – Dog & Puppy Tips
presented by Joe Inglis

For more information about currently available
and forthcoming book and DVD titles please visit:

www.thegreatestintheworld.com

The GREATEST
in the WORLD

or write to:

The Greatest in the World Ltd
PO Box 3182
Stratford-upon-Avon
Warwickshire CV37 7XW
United Kingdom

Tel / Fax: +44(0)1789 299616
Email: info@thegreatestintheworld.com

The author

Malcolm Boyden is a double Sony award winning radio presenter. He was voted Britain's Radio Personality of the Year in 1997, and followed that up in 2001 with a Broadcaster of the Year accolade.

Malcolm currently presents a series of popular programmes on BBC radio across the Midlands and is a regular on BBC Five Live. He also writes for The Times newspaper and, as a published author, has three books to his credit.

Malcolm has appeared in many successful stage productions, including pantomime, alongside stars such as Frank Bruno and Julian Clary. He's even turned out for the Royal Ballet!